What to Consider When You're Considering Divorce:

A Practical Guide to Navigating the First Steps Moving Forward

Genevieve "Jenny" Dreizen

Olivia Dreizen Howell

FIRST EDITION

This book was set in 10-14 pt. Times New Roman

by Fresh Starts Registry

ISBN 979-8-9881059-8-5

Published by Fresh Starts Registry

Distributed by Fresh Starts Registry

FreshStartsRegistry.com

Please note: This book is not intended to provide legal advice or replace professional legal counsel. It is a supportive, informational guide designed to help you feel more organized, empowered, and prepared as you navigate your divorce journey. Every situation is unique, and while this workbook offers tools, checklists, and general guidance, it is not a substitute for advice from a licensed attorney or financial professional. Use this book as a companion to your process—not as a legal directive—and always consult the appropriate experts for decisions specific to your case.

Welcome, we're so glad you're here.

*We're really proud of you
for making a brave choice.*

Hey there,

Before we dive in, we want you to feel completely comfortable with this book. If the title feels too bold or you'd prefer a bit more privacy, just send us an email at hi@freshstartsregistry. com with your address, and we'll send you a discreet, no-fuss sticker to cover it up. Your comfort matters to us, always.

— The Fresh Starts Team

Contents

Introduction:

If you're holding this book, it's probably because you're considering divorce. If so, we want you to know two things right from the start: first, we are incredibly proud of you for even allowing yourself to think about what you truly need; and second, from this point on, you are not alone. For many people, the journey of contemplating divorce isn't a quick decision—it's a process that can take months, even years. It's quiet moments of wondering if things will ever change, late-night Google searches about how much it costs to live alone, and deep breaths before hard conversations. We know this stage well, and we are here to guide you through it.

The decision to consider divorce is often the hardest part. It's the weight of imagining two different paths and not knowing which one holds more peace. It's the swirl of questions: What if I regret it? How will this affect the kids? Can I afford to do this on my own? What does life even look like on the other side? If you've been wrestling with these thoughts, you are absolutely not alone. Most people consider divorce for a long time—sometimes years—before they actually take steps forward. And that's okay. Taking time to understand what you want, what you need, and what the possibilities are is an act of courage and care, not one of indecision.

That's why we created this book as a guide for you in the consideration stage. It's designed to be your companion as you navigate the questions and emotions that come with even thinking about the possibility of divorce. We understand how isolating and overwhelming this stage can feel, and we also know that having the right support and information can make all the difference. Our mission at Fresh Starts has always been to provide a roadmap for people navigating major life changes, and this book is no different. Whether you decide to stay and rebuild or move forward toward a new chapter, we want you to feel informed, supported, and above all, not alone.

Throughout this book, we will walk you through the things you should consider during this time of contemplation. We'll talk about understanding your financial readiness and knowing how to prepare for the financial realities of single living. We'll guide you through the legal landscape, explaining what steps you might need to take if you decide to move forward. We'll navigate conversations with your partner, children, and loved ones with empathy and clarity, making sure you feel prepared for what's ahead. We'll discuss self-care strategies to maintain your emotional health during this deeply personal time.

And finally, we'll help you explore your own desires and long-term vision for your life, so you can step into your next chapter with confidence.

Our hope is that by the end of this book, you will have clarity and confidence in whatever path you choose. This is your journey, and you deserve to feel empowered and supported every step of the way. Take a deep breath, pour yourself a cup of something warm, and let's start exploring what comes next. You've got this—and we're right here with you.

CHAPTER 1

What to Consider Before You Even Begin to Consider Divorce

Before you even allow yourself to utter the word "divorce," there are quiet, almost imperceptible shifts that happen. Maybe it's a slow erosion of joy in your everyday life, a gnawing feeling that the life you're living isn't quite your own, or the realization that the things you once ignored now feel impossible to accept. For many people, thoughts of divorce begin long before any real consideration takes place. It's a whisper, a flicker of doubt, a moment of clarity that's quickly tucked away. This chapter is about giving space to those whispers, not to rush into decisions, but to honor the fact that they are speaking to you for a reason.

If you're here, reading this, it's likely because those whispers have grown louder. You might be at the point where you're researching what life could look like on your own, or maybe you're just starting to wonder if the things you've been accepting as normal are really acceptable. And that's where this journey begins— with acknowledgment. It's the brave and terrifying act of saying, I'm not sure if I can live like this anymore. That statement alone is powerful. It's the first crack of light in what may have been a long, dark tunnel.

Before you move any further, it's important to understand that contemplating divorce is not about being impulsive or reactionary. It's about honoring the thoughts that have likely been with you for quite some time. It's about getting real with yourself about what's working, what's not, and what you've been tolerating. To even begin this process with clarity, there are foundational things you should consider first.

1. Are You Truly Unhappy, or Are You Unfulfilled?

It's crucial to understand the difference between unhappiness and unfulfillment. Unhappiness is situational; it's reactive. Unfulfillment is deeper; it's a lingering sense that something essential is missing. Before you even think about what divorce would look like, it's important to distinguish between the two. Sometimes, unfulfillment can be addressed within the marriage through therapy, self-reflection, or changes in behavior. Other times, it's a signal that your path is diverging from your partner's, and that's okay.

2. What Does Your Support System Look Like?

Before you even think about considering divorce, take stock of your support system. Who do you have in your life that you can turn to? Friends? Family? A therapist? Contemplating such a massive change is nearly impossible to do in isolation. Having people who can provide perspective, support, and even a shoulder to cry on can make all the difference.

Find the Experts you need at freshstartsregistry.com/experts

3. Have You Been Honest with Yourself?

The first person you need to be honest with is yourself. If you're here, you've probably been doing a lot of rationalizing. It's not that bad. Things will get better. I can handle this. But now is the time to truly reflect. Are you happy? Are you fulfilled? Are you living the life you imagined for yourself? This isn't about blame or guilt; it's about clarity.

4. Do You Understand Your Financial Situation?

Money is one of the biggest barriers to divorce, and it's important to understand where you stand financially before you even begin to consider what leaving might look like. Do you know how much debt you have? Do you understand your household expenses? Taking an honest look at your finances now will save you heartache later.

5. Are You Prepared to Ask Hard Questions?

Before you even begin to consider divorce, you need to be ready to ask yourself—and answer—some incredibly hard questions. What do you want your life to look like? What are you willing to compromise on? What are your non-negotiable? These questions might not have easy answers, but beginning to ask them now will set you on the path to clarity.

6. Are You Ready to Imagine a Different Life?

It's one thing to be unhappy where you are; it's another to allow yourself to imagine something different. Before you even begin to consider divorce, try to imagine your life without the marriage. What would it look like? What would change? What would stay the same? Sometimes the biggest barrier to change is the fear of the unknown.

Moving Forward

If you're nodding along, feeling seen and understood, that's because we've been where you are. These first steps of honest reflection are the most important ones. Before you move forward, make sure you've considered these six foundational questions. They will serve as your compass as you begin to navigate this incredibly personal and transformative journey. And remember: you are not alone in this. We're right here with you, every step of the way.

CHAPTER 2

Understanding Your Financial Landscape

One of the biggest barriers to divorce is financial uncertainty. It's often the reason many people stay longer in marriages that aren't serving them—because the fear of financial instability can feel insurmountable. But here's the truth: understanding your financial landscape before you make any decisions can empower you to move forward with confidence, no matter which path you choose. In this chapter, we're going to break down the essential questions you need to ask yourself, why these questions matter, and the steps you can take to gain clarity and control over your financial situation.

What Do You Own?

Before you can understand where you stand financially, you need a clear picture of what you own. This includes your home, cars, jewelry, valuable collections, and even digital assets like cryptocurrency. The reason this question is so important is that when it comes to divorce, everything that is considered marital property is subject to division. Knowing what you own—both individually and as a couple— gives you the foundation to understand what might be at stake.

Action Step: Take an afternoon to list out every major asset you can think of. Walk through your home, open up your bank accounts, and pull out any documents that show ownership of property or valuables. Create a simple document that lists everything you own, its approximate value, and whether it's in your name, your partner's name, or both.

ASSET INVENTORY

Your inventory should include but is not limited to the below.

Real Property: Marital home, Condominium, Vacation home(s), Business property, Rental property, Undeveloped land

Personal Property: Home furnishings, Appliances, Rugs, Antiques, Artwork, China, Crystal, Precious metals, Coin collections, Sporting Equipment, Tools, Collectibles, Guns, Computers, Laptops, Tablets, Cellular Phones, Home office equipment, jewelry, clothing, Furs, Motor vehicles,, Motorcycles Boats, Campers, Recreational vehicles, ATVs

Financial Assets: Cash on hand, Checking accounts, Savings accounts, Money market accounts, Certificates of deposit, Christmas club accounts, Educational accounts, Retirement accounts, 401(k) plans, Pensions, Profit sharing, IRAs, Stocks and bonds, Mutual funds, Certificates of deposit, Cryptocurrency and NFT, Annuities, Cash value of life insurance policy, Trusts

ASSET INVENTORY

ASSET	DESCRIPTION	CATEGORY	VALUE

Date: _____   **Page_____of_____**

Find the Experts you need at freshstartsregistry.com/experts

ASSET INVENTORY

ASSET	DESCRIPTION	CATEGORY	VALUE

Date: _____   **Page**_____ **of** _____

What Do You Owe?

Just as important as understanding what you own is knowing what you owe. This includes credit card debt, mortgages, car loans, student loans, and any other liabilities. This question matters because debt is often divided in divorce, and understanding your obligations now will help you prepare for what that might look like moving forward.

Action Step: Pull your credit report and write down every line of debt you have. Include the total amount owed, the monthly payments, and whose name is on the account. If you share debt with your partner, make a note of it, as this will impact the division process.

Debt Tracking Worksheet

Instructions: Use this worksheet to track every line of debt you discover in your credit report. Include all relevant information to help you understand what you owe and how it may be divided.

Checklist Before You Start:

☐ Pull your credit report from all three bureaus (Experian, Equifax, TransUnion).

☐ Highlight or note each line of credit or loan.

☐ Review for accuracy—dispute anything that doesn't look right.

Note whether debts are joint or individual—this will impact legal/financial planning.

Debt Tracking Worksheet

Creditor Name	Type of Debt (e.g., credit card, loan, mortgage)	Total Amount Owed	Monthly Payment	Name(s) on Account	Joint or Individual?	Notes (e.g., in use, closed, disputed)

Debt Tracking Worksheet

Creditor Name	Type of Debt (e.g., credit card, loan, mortgage)	Total Amount Owed	Monthly Payment	Name(s) on Account	Joint or Individual?	Notes (e.g., in use, closed, disputed)

Find the Experts you need at freshstartsregistry.com/experts

How Much Do You Spend Every Month?

One of the most eye-opening parts of understanding your financial landscape is truly knowing how much you spend each month. From mortgage or rent payments to groceries, childcare, and personal expenses, it's crucial to get clear on what your lifestyle costs. This is important because after divorce, your income and expenses will look different. Preparing for that change now can make all the difference.

Action Step: Go through your bank statements and credit card statements for the past three months. Write down every expense—yes, even the little ones like coffee and streaming services. Average it out to understand your monthly spending. This is your baseline.

———

Monthly Spending Baseline Worksheet

Instructions: Go through your bank and credit card statements for the past 3 months. Log every single expense, big or small, in the table below. Assign categories to each, from the category bank below. Once filled in, calculate your monthly average in each category to get your baseline.

Rent/Mortgage	Subscriptions/Streaming
Utilities (Gas, Electric, Water)	Kids/Childcare
Groceries	Medical/Health Expenses
Dining Out/Coffee	Shopping (Clothes, Gifts, etc.)
Transportation (Gas, Rail, Uber)	Personal Care (Salon, Nails)
Insurance (Health, Auto, etc.)	Entertainment/Recreation

Month 1

AMOUNT	DESCRIPTION	CATEGORY

Date: _____   **Page**_____ **of** _____

Find the Experts you need at freshstartsregistry.com/experts

Month 1

AMOUNT	DESCRIPTION	CATEGORY

Date: _____   **Page_____ of _____**

Month 2

AMOUNT	DESCRIPTION	CATEGORY

Date: _____   **Page** _____ **of** _____

Find the Experts you need at freshstartsregistry.com/experts

Month 2

AMOUNT	*DESCRIPTION*	*CATEGORY*

Date: _____   **Page_____ of_____**

Month 3

AMOUNT	DESCRIPTION	CATEGORY

Date: _____   **Page** _____ **of** _____

Find the Experts you need at freshstartsregistry.com/experts

Month 3

AMOUNT	DESCRIPTION	CATEGORY

Date: _____   **Page_____ of _____**

3 Month Review

CATEGORY	MONTH 1 TOTAL:	MONTH 2 TOTAL:	MONTH 3 TOTAL:	3 MONTH AVERAGE
Rent/Mortgage				
Utilities (Gas, Electric, Water)				
Groceries				
Dining Out/Coffee				
Transportation (Gas, Rail, Uber)				
Insurance (Health, Auto, etc.)				
Subscriptions/ Streaming				
Kids/Childcare				
Medical/Health Expenses				
Shopping (Clothes, Gifts, etc.)				
Personal Care (Salon, Nails)				
Entertainment/ Recreation				
Total				

Find the Experts you need at freshstartsregistry.com/experts

What Is Your Income?

When you're considering divorce, it's important to understand exactly how much money is coming in each month. This includes not only your salary but any bonuses, investments, rental income, or side gigs. Knowing your income allows you to realistically evaluate your financial independence and the steps you need to take moving forward.

Action Step: Gather your most recent pay stubs, tax returns, and any documentation for additional income. Add it all up and understand what your true monthly income is after taxes and deductions.

Are There Joint Accounts?

Joint bank accounts, credit cards, and investments are often shared between spouses. Before you can make any decisions, it's critical to know where those accounts are, how much is in them, and who has access. This is important because changes to these accounts can happen rapidly during the divorce process, sometimes without warning.

Action Step: Create a list of every joint account you share with your partner. Take note of the balances and recent activity. If you suspect there might be accounts you aren't aware of, now is the time to look deeper.

What Are Your Financial Goals?

Understanding your financial landscape isn't just about what you have now; it's also about where you want to go. Are you hoping to buy your own home? Do you want to go back to school? Knowing your goals will help you understand what kind of financial stability you need post-divorce.

Action Step: Take some time to journal about what you want your financial life to look like in five years. What do you want to have? What do you want to be free from? This vision will serve as your compass as you move forward.

1. **Five years from now, what does financial peace look and feel like for you?**
   (Describe your daily life, your habits, your home, and how money flows in and out.)

2. **What burdens—financial or emotional—do you want to be free from by then?**
   (Think about debt, stress, guilt, generational patterns, or scarcity mindsets.)

3. **What would having financial freedom allow you to do, give, or become?**
   (Explore the possibilities—career changes, travel, rest, generosity, legacy.)

Moving Forward

Understanding your financial landscape is one of the most empowering things you can do before even considering divorce. When you know what you own, what you owe, how much you spend, and where you want to go, you take back control. You're no longer moving forward in the dark—you're making informed, empowered decisions. And that's the foundation for whatever comes next. Take some time to answer these questions, and we know it can be hard, but it will help you feel more confident in your decision making process as we keep going.

CHAPTER 3

Navigating the Legal Landscape

Divorce is about so much more than heartbreak—it's also about paperwork, decisions, and setting yourself up for the next chapter. The legal stuff might feel overwhelming, but it's so important—because what gets decided during this process will shape your money, your parenting, and your peace of mind moving forward. We want you to feel informed, not intimidated. In this chapter, we'll walk you through the key questions to ask, why they matter, and how to get organized before you meet with a lawyer—so you can walk in feeling prepared, grounded, and totally in your power.

What Type of Divorce is Right for Me?

The first question to ask yourself is what type of divorce you are considering. There are several different ways to approach divorce, including uncontested, contested, collaborative, and mediated. Understanding the differences is crucial because each one has its own legal implications, costs, and timelines. An uncontested divorce, where both parties agree on terms, is often the quickest and least expensive. A contested divorce involves disagreements that may require court intervention. Collaborative divorce focuses on negotiation outside of court with legal support, while mediation involves a neutral third party to help reach agreements.

Action Step: Research the different types of divorce available in your state. Write down the pros and cons of each and think about which option aligns best with your current situation and your goals moving forward.

Do I Understand Custody Arrangements?

If you have children, one of the most critical legal aspects of divorce is determining custody arrangements. This can include physical custody (where the children live), legal custody (who makes major decisions for them), and visitation schedules. Understanding the options—like joint custody, sole custody, and shared parenting— will help you enter conversations prepared. It's important to know what is standard in your state and what is realistic given your current living situation.

Action Step: Take time to learn about custody laws in your state. Reflect on your children's needs and your capacity to meet them. Think about what kind of arrangement would be best for your children emotionally and practically, and be ready to discuss this with your attorney.

Find the Experts you need at freshstartsregistry.com/experts

What Will Happen with Our Property?

Property division is a significant part of the legal landscape of divorce. Understanding how property is divided, whether through community property laws or equitable distribution, is key. Community property states generally split marital assets 50/50, while equitable distribution states divide property based on what is fair but not necessarily equal. This includes real estate, bank accounts, vehicles, and even household items. Knowing what to expect can help you advocate for your fair share.

Action Step: Begin compiling a list of all marital property, including your home, vehicles, savings, and investments. Note which items were acquired before the marriage, as these may be considered separate property. This list will be crucial when discussing property division with your attorney.

Marital Property Inventory Worksheet

Instructions: Use this worksheet to list all assets acquired during the marriage and any you owned before it. Be as detailed as possible—this list will be incredibly helpful during legal and financial conversations.

Property Categories to Consider:

Primary residence

Vacation home or timeshares

Vehicles (cars, motorcycles, RVs)

Bank accounts (checking, savings)

Retirement accounts (401(k), IRA)

Stocks, bonds, and investments

Businesses

Collectibles, jewelry, or valuables

Furniture and household items

Marital Property Inventory Worksheet *Page_____ of _____*

Item Description	Category	Estimated Value	Date Acquired	Owned Before Marriage? (Y/N)	In Whose Name(s)?	Notes (e.g., mortgage, loan, location)

Find the Experts you need at freshstartsregistry.com/experts

Marital Property Inventory Worksheet   *Page_____ of _____*

Item Description	Category	Estimated Value	Date Acquired	Owned Before Marriage? (Y/N)	In Whose Name(s)?	Notes (e.g., mortgage, loan, location)

Marital Property Inventory Worksheet

Item Description	Category	Estimated Value	Date Acquired	Owned Before Marriage? (Y/N)	In Whose Name(s)?	Notes (e.g., mortgage, loan, location)

Find the Experts you need at freshstartsregistry.com/experts

Do I Need a Lawyer or Can I Handle This Myself?

One of the biggest questions many people ask is whether they need a lawyer. The answer depends on your situation. If your divorce is amicable and straightforward, you might consider a DIY divorce or mediation. However, if there are significant assets, complicated custody arrangements, or if your partner is uncooperative, hiring a lawyer may be essential. Understanding the cost implications and the role a lawyer plays can help you make the right decision.

Action Step: Research family law attorneys in your area and consider booking a consultation. Even if you are contemplating mediation or a DIY divorce, understanding your rights from a legal professional can be incredibly valuable.

Am I Prepared for the Legal Process?

Divorce is not a single event; it's a process. There are filings, negotiations, hearings, and, sometimes, court appearances. Being prepared means understanding the steps ahead of you and knowing what documents you'll need—like financial statements, proof of income, and lists of assets and debts. Knowing what to expect can ease your anxiety and give you a clearer path forward.

Action Step: Create a folder—digital or physical—where you can begin collecting important documents. Start with your marriage certificate, bank statements, mortgage information, and recent tax returns. This will serve as your foundation when you begin the legal process.

Moving Forward

Navigating the legal landscape of divorce is challenging, but it's also empowering when you know what to expect. Asking yourself the right questions, understanding the different types of divorce, knowing your rights around custody and property, and preparing for the legal process can transform uncertainty into confidence. The more informed you are, the more you can advocate for yourself and your future.

CHAPTER 4

———

Finding the Right Attorney and Legal Representation

Before you start Googling divorce attorneys at midnight (we've been there), let's take a breath and talk about what really matters: feeling supported, informed, and in control. Divorce is a legal process, yes—but it's also personal, and the lawyer you choose can shape your entire experience. You deserve someone who sees the full picture: your rights, your needs, your future. In this chapter, we'll help you figure out what to look for, which questions to ask, and how to find legal support that feels less intimidating and more like a true teammate.

And remember, if you want a deeper dive into these questions, check out our free e-book Your Divorce Support Team: 250+ Questions to Help You Build Your Divorce Support Team for everything you need to know about hiring a lawyer and building your team.

––––––––

What Type of Lawyer Do I Need?

The first step in finding the right attorney is understanding the kind of legal support you need. Divorce law can be incredibly specific, with some attorneys specializing in mediation, collaborative divorce, high-net-worth divorces, or custody battles. Asking yourself what you anticipate your divorce to look like—whether amicable, contested, or highly complex—will help you identify the kind of lawyer who is best suited to support you.

Questions to Ask: Do you specialize in divorce law specifically? What percentage of your practice is dedicated to family law? Have you handled cases similar to mine before?

Action Step: Head to FreshStartsRegistry.com and begin by researching family law attorneys in your area. Look for those who specialize in the type of divorce you are considering. Make a list of at least three to five potential attorneys and book initial consultations to get a feel for their experience and approach.

What Are Your Legal Options?

Not all divorces look the same, and not all require the same legal intervention. You may want to pursue mediation, where you and your spouse work with a neutral third party to reach agreements. Alternatively, you might consider collaborative divorce, which emphasizes cooperation and avoids the courtroom. Understanding your options can save you time, money, and emotional energy.

Questions to Ask: What are the pros and cons of mediation versus litigation? How does collaborative divorce work, and is it a good option for me? Are there alternative dispute resolution methods that might be right for my case?

Action Step: Research the different types of divorce processes. Take notes on what seems to fit best with your situation, and be ready to discuss these options during your consultations.

How Will Communication Be Handled?

One of the most important aspects of working with an attorney is clear communication. You should know how often you can expect updates, how you will be billed for communication, and who your primary contact will be. This prevents misunderstandings and keeps you informed throughout the process.

Questions to Ask: How often will you update me on the status of my case? Will I be communicating mostly with you or with a paralegal? What is your preferred method of communication—email, phone, or in-person meetings?

Action Step: During your consultations, take note of how responsive and clear each attorney is in their communication. If you find yourself waiting too long for responses or receiving unclear information, that could be a sign of how things will proceed if you hire them.

Divorce Lawyer Questionnaire

1. **How long have you been practicing family law?** The length of time a lawyer has been practicing family law is an important factor to consider. You want to ensure that your lawyer has significant experience in handling divorce cases. Ask them how long they've been practicing family law, and what percentage of their cases are related to divorce. You should also ask about their success rate in handling divorce cases.

2. **What is your area of expertise?** Some lawyers specialize in certain areas of family law, such as child custody, divorce mediation, or collaborative law. If you have a specific issue that you need help with, it is important to find a lawyer who has experience in that area.

Divorce Lawyer Questionnaire

3. **Will you be the primary attorney on my case?** Some law firms have multiple attorneys, and it's essential to know who will be handling your case. Ask the lawyer if they will be the primary attorney on your case, or if someone else will be handling it. If someone else will be handling it, ask to meet with that attorney before signing a contract.

4. **What is your fee structure?** Lawyers typically charge by the hour or on a retainer basis. It is important to understand how much you will be charged before you hire a lawyer. Ask about their hourly rate, how they bill for their services, and what their retainer fee is. You should also ask about any additional fees that may arise during the divorce process.

5. **How will you communicate with me?** It is important to find a lawyer who is responsive to your calls and emails. You should also ask how often you can expect to meet with your lawyer.

6. **What is your availability?** It's crucial to know how available your lawyer will be during the divorce process. Ask about their availability and how they communicate with their clients. Do they respond promptly to emails and phone calls? Will they be available for in-person meetings if needed?

7. **What is your approach to divorce?** Some lawyers take a more aggressive approach to divorce, while others prefer to negotiate a settlement. It is important to find a lawyer who is willing to work with you to achieve your goals.

8. **Can you provide me with references?** Asking for references is a great way to get feedback from other clients about a lawyer's experience and representation.

9. **Do you feel comfortable representing me?** It is important to feel comfortable with your lawyer and to have confidence in their ability to represent you. If you do not feel comfortable with a lawyer, it is okay to find someone else.

10. **What is your experience with alternative dispute resolution options?** Ask about the lawyer's experience with alternative dispute resolution methods like mediation or collaborative divorce. Understanding their willingness to explore these options can be beneficial in achieving a more amicable resolution.

Find the Experts you need at freshstartsregistry.com/experts

What Are the Costs Involved?

Legal representation is an investment, and understanding the costs upfront is crucial. Some attorneys work on retainer, others bill hourly, and some may have fixed rates for specific services. Ask about all potential fees, including court costs, administrative fees, and potential extra charges.

Questions to Ask: What is your retainer fee, and what does it cover? Do you bill hourly, and if so, what is your rate? Are there any additional fees I should be aware of?

Action Step: Ask for a clear breakdown of costs during your consultation and request a written estimate if possible. Compare costs between your top choices and understand exactly what each payment covers.

Are You Comfortable Advocating for My Needs?

Your attorney is your advocate, and they should be willing to fight for what matters to you. Whether it's custody arrangements, property division, or spousal support, your attorney should understand your priorities and be committed to representing them.

Questions to Ask: How do you handle high-conflict cases? Are you comfortable advocating for my specific needs and concerns? How do you approach negotiations versus going to trial?

Action Step: Reflect on your priorities before you meet with attorneys. Be honest about what matters most to you and make sure your potential lawyer is confident in advocating for those needs.

Moving Forward

Finding the right attorney is about more than just legal representation; it's about feeling confident and supported during one of the most challenging transitions of your life. Take your time, ask the right questions, and make sure the person you choose is truly in your corner. And remember, for even more detailed guidance, check out our free e-book Your Divorce Support Team: 250+ Questions to Help You Build Your Divorce Support Team. The right support team can make all the difference.

Find the Experts you need at freshstartsregistry.com/experts

CHAPTER 5

———

Understanding Spousal Support and Alimony

One of the most commonly misunderstood aspects of divorce is spousal support, also known as alimony. This financial support is designed to help the lower-earning spouse maintain a reasonable standard of living post-divorce. The idea behind alimony is to provide some level of financial balance, especially if one partner sacrificed career growth or earning potential to support the family. Understanding how spousal support is determined, how long it lasts, and how it's enforced can help you better prepare for what lies ahead.

Am I Eligible for Spousal Support?

The first question to ask yourself is whether you are eligible to receive spousal support—or if you may be required to pay it. Eligibility often depends on a range of factors, including the length of the marriage, the financial disparity between you and your spouse, and your ability to earn a living independently. Courts also consider age, health, and contributions to the household or family business.

Questions to Ask: How long were we married? Is there a significant difference in our incomes? Did I leave my career or reduce my work hours to support the family?

Action Step: Review your financial situation and compare it to your spouse's. Take note of any gaps in income or work history that might impact eligibility. If you suspect alimony may be part of your divorce, consult your state's guidelines for spousal support calculations.

How is Spousal Support Calculated?

Understanding how spousal support is calculated can help you set realistic expectations. While the exact formula varies by state, most courts consider income, living expenses, and the standard of living during the marriage. Some states have specific formulas, while others give judges more discretion to decide based on the individual circumstances of the marriage.

Questions to Ask: What formula does my state use to determine spousal support? Are factors like debt, cost of living, and childcare expenses considered? Is my state a community property or equitable distribution state?

Action Step: Research the laws in your state to understand how alimony is calculated. If possible, consult with a financial advisor or attorney who can walk you through the numbers so you can be better prepared.

How Long Will Spousal Support Last?

Another important consideration is the duration of spousal support. Some payments are temporary, designed to help the lower-earning spouse get back on their feet. Others are long-term or even permanent, depending on the circumstances. Courts will often set a time limit based on the length of the marriage, but certain conditions—like disability or lack of career history—might extend the timeframe.

Questions to Ask: Does my state have guidelines for the duration of spousal support? Are there specific events that could trigger an end to support, such as remarriage? Can the amount or duration be modified if circumstances change?

Action Step: Find out what your state laws say about the duration of alimony. Create a financial plan based on the potential length of payments, whether you are the recipient or the payer.

Can Spousal Support Be Modified?

It's important to understand that spousal support is not always set in stone. Changes in circumstances—like job loss, remarriage, or a significant shift in income—can sometimes lead to modifications. However, the process for modification varies by state and can require legal action.

Questions to Ask: What is the process for modifying spousal support in my state? Do I need to go back to court to make changes? What types of changes qualify for a modification?

Action Step: If you suspect your financial situation may change, familiarize yourself with your state's modification process. Keep documentation of any significant changes that could impact your ability to pay or receive support.

Moving Forward

Understanding spousal support is key to preparing for life after divorce. Whether you're the one paying or receiving, knowing how it's calculated, how long it lasts, and the conditions for modification will help you create a realistic plan for your financial future. Take the time to understand your rights and responsibilities so you can move forward with clarity and confidence.

Alimony Estimator Worksheet

Purpose: This worksheet will help you organize financial details, understand what impacts support amounts, and estimate what spousal support (alimony) may look like in your case. We recommend Googling "Alimony + your state" to learn the likelihood and conditions of alimony as well as calculate what might be owed.

Length of Marriage (Years): _____

Is Alimony Likely in Your State?

☐ **Yes** ☐ **No** ☐ **Maybe (check with your lawyer)**

Factors Considered in Your State (Check All):

☐ **Length of marriage**

☐ **Difference in income**

☐ **One spouse stayed home with children**

☐ **Age or health of either spouse**

☐ **Education or work history gaps**

☐ **Marital standard of living**

Estimate Monthly Alimony (if applicable): $_____

Proposed Duration (in months or years): _____

Find the Experts you need at freshstartsregistry.com/experts

Notes & Legal Follow-Up

Questions to Ask a Lawyer or Mediator:

How does alimony get negotiated in my situation?

Next Steps:

☐ Schedule a meeting with a family lawyer

☐ Research your state's support guidelines

☐ Gather pay stubs, tax returns, and bank statements

☐ Prepare for mediation or court

_____

_____

_____

_____

_____

_____

_____

CHAPTER 6

———

What to Consider if You're Considering Filing a DIY Divorce

When it comes to divorce, many people are drawn to the idea of handling the process themselves. A DIY divorce, or Do-It-Yourself divorce, is one where you manage the paperwork, filing, and negotiations without the involvement of an attorney. While this path can be more affordable and straightforward in some cases, it's important to understand what you're signing up for before you decide to go it alone. In this chapter, we'll break down the questions you need to ask, why they matter, and the steps to take if you choose to handle your divorce on your own.

Is a DIY Divorce Right for Me?

The first and most important question to ask yourself is whether a DIY divorce is right for your specific situation. DIY divorces are typically best suited for couples who are largely in agreement about major issues like property division, child custody, and financial arrangements. If your divorce is contested or involves complicated assets, a DIY approach may not be the best option.

Questions to Ask: Are my spouse and I in agreement about how to divide our assets? Is there mutual understanding around custody and parenting time? Are our finances relatively straightforward?

Action Step: Take an honest assessment of your current situation. Write down the major areas of your divorce—property, finances, custody—and make note of where you and your spouse are aligned and where there might be disagreements. This will help you evaluate whether a DIY approach is realistic.

Do I Understand My State's Divorce Laws?

Divorce laws vary greatly from state to state, and understanding the requirements where you live is crucial if you're planning to file on your own. Some states require a waiting period, others need specific paperwork, and all have their own guidelines for property division and custody arrangements. Knowing what is legally required will prevent unnecessary delays and complications.

Questions to Ask: What are the legal requirements for filing for divorce in my state? Is there a mandatory waiting period? What documents do I need to complete the process?

Action Step: Visit your state's government website or local courthouse to find specific guidelines and requirements for divorce. Print out or save the necessary forms and begin familiarizing yourself with the steps involved.

Am I Prepared to Handle the Paperwork?

One of the biggest challenges of a DIY divorce is managing the paperwork. Filing for divorce requires submitting the right forms, often multiple times, and keeping track of deadlines. Errors in paperwork can cause delays or even affect the outcome of your divorce.

Questions to Ask: Am I comfortable completing legal forms accurately? Do I understand the deadlines and filing requirements? Do I have a plan for submitting and tracking these documents?

Action Step: Organize a folder—physical or digital—where you can keep all forms, copies of documents, and important dates. Create a checklist to track your progress and deadlines.

Do I Understand the Risks of a DIY Divorce?

While a DIY divorce can be cost-effective, it also comes with risks. If you miss a critical detail or misunderstand your rights, it could impact your financial security, custody arrangements, or property division. Understanding the limitations of going solo is vital before you commit to this path.

Questions to Ask: What are the risks of representing myself in my divorce? What happens if I make a mistake in the paperwork? Am I prepared to negotiate directly with my spouse?

Action Step: Research common mistakes people make during DIY divorces. Consider consulting with an attorney for a one-time review of your documents before you submit them. This small step can save you from costly errors.

Moving Forward

A DIY divorce can be a powerful way to take control of your situation and save money, but it's not right for everyone. The key is understanding your situation clearly, knowing your state's laws, and being honest with yourself about the complexity of your divorce. If you decide to pursue this path, preparation and organization are your best allies. Take the time to fully understand each step, and don't be afraid to seek help if you need it.

CHAPTER 7

Understanding the Legal Process and Court Appearances

Divorce isn't one big moment—it's a process that unfolds over time, with lots of steps along the way. And while the legal side of things can feel intimidating, understanding how it all works can take some of the fear out of it. From dividing up property to sorting out custody and support, there's a structure to it—and knowing what to expect (and what's expected of you) can make everything feel a little more manageable. We're here to help you walk through it with clarity, not chaos.

What Are the Steps in the Divorce Process?

The first thing to understand is that divorce is a step-by-step process. While each case is unique, most divorces follow a general pattern: filing a petition, serving your spouse, waiting for a response, negotiating terms, and finalizing the agreement. If both parties are in agreement, the process can be relatively smooth. If not, court appearances and negotiations become part of the journey.

Questions to Ask: What are the specific steps in my state for filing for divorce? How long does each stage typically take? Are there mandatory waiting periods I should be aware of?

Action Step: Research the divorce process in your state. Create a timeline to visualize each step so you know what to expect as you move forward. Understanding the timeline can help manage expectations and reduce anxiety.

What Happens During Court Appearances?

Court appearances may be part of your divorce process, especially if there are disagreements over custody, property, or financial arrangements. It's important to know what to expect when you enter the courtroom—how to present yourself, what documents you may need, and what types of questions you might be asked.

Questions to Ask: What should I bring to my court appearance? How should I prepare to speak to the judge? Will I need to provide documentation during the hearing?

Action Step: If you anticipate court appearances, prepare by gathering all relevant documentation—bank statements, mortgage information, proof of income, and custody agreements. Practice how you will present your side of the case, and consider attending a local court session to observe the process.

Court Prep Worksheet

What should I bring to my court appearance?

Check the items off as you gather them and store them in one central place (a physical folder or a digital option like Google Drive or Dropbox is a good idea!)

Personal Identification & Vital Records

- ☐ Photo ID (driver's license, passport)

- ☐ Social Security cards (yours and your children's)

- ☐ Marriage certificate

- ☐ Birth certificates (for you, your spouse, and children)

- ☐ Immigration documents (if applicable)

Financial Records

- ☐ Recent pay stubs (yours and your spouse's)

- ☐ Tax returns (past 2–3 years, personal and joint)

- ☐ Bank statements (checking, savings, credit union accounts)

- ☐ Retirement account statements (401(k), IRA, pension plans)

- ☐ Investment account statements (stocks, bonds, crypto, etc.)

- ☐ Credit card statements (individual and joint)

- ☐ Loan documents (mortgage, student, auto, personal)

- ☐ List of all debts and liabilities

- ☐ Proof of assets (valuable possessions, collectibles, etc.)

Court Prep Worksheet

Housing & Property Records

- ☐ Lease agreement or mortgage documents

- ☐ Property deed(s)

- ☐ Property tax statements

- ☐ Utility bills (proof of residence or to establish living arrangements)

- ☐ Home appraisal or market analysis (if available)

- ☐ Insurance & Healthcare

Health insurance policy documents

- ☐ Life insurance policies (individual and employer-provided)

- ☐ Auto and home/renters insurance documents

- ☐ List of current prescriptions and healthcare providers

- ☐ Medical bills and expenses

Legal Documents

- ☐ Prenuptial or postnuptial agreements (if applicable)

- ☐ Previous court orders or judgments (including from other cases)

- ☐ Custody or parenting agreements (formal or informal)

- ☐ Protective or restraining orders

- ☐ Documentation of any abuse or unsafe situations (photos, messages, police reports)

Court Prep Worksheet

Parenting & Custody

- ☐ School records or report cards
- ☐ Childcare or tuition payment records
- ☐ Extracurricular or special needs documentation
- ☐ Communication logs between you and your co-parent
- ☐ Proposed parenting plan or custody schedule

Communication & Evidence (if needed)

- ☐ Emails, texts, or messages relevant to your case
- ☐ Calendar of parenting time or major incidents
- ☐ Journal or timeline of events

Optional But Helpful

- ☐ Divorce petition or response paperwork
- ☐ Financial affidavit or disclosure forms
- ☐ Budget worksheet (current and projected)
- ☐ Witness list (if applicable)

Tip: Make copies of everything. Keep one set organized in a binder or folder for yourself and bring an extra set for the court or your lawyer. Some courts may require digital submissions too.

How should I prepare to speak to the judge?

What are the 2–3 main points you want to communicate clearly?

Point 1:

_____

_____

_____

_____

Point 2:

_____

_____

_____

Point 3:

_____

_____

_____

_____

Practice presenting your case out loud:

Try talking it through in the mirror or with a friend. Keep it clear, calm, and focused on facts.

Optional but empowering:

☐ Attend a local court session to observe

☐ Research your judge or courthouse online

☐ Plan what you'll wear and how you'll get there

Dress with Respect for the Courtroom

Aim for business casual or slightly more formal. Think of what you'd wear to a job interview or a parent-teacher conference.

Avoid anything too revealing, flashy, or informal (no crop tops, ripped jeans, flip-flops, or slogan tees).

If you're not sure, lean toward conservative and simple: clean lines, neutral colors, closed-toe shoes.

Wear Something That Grounds You

Choose something that makes you feel confident and calm—not a costume, but something that feels like you.

If you have a piece of jewelry or clothing that brings comfort or emotional strength, wear it (as long as it's subtle).

Consider How You'll Be Perceived

Judges and court staff may unconsciously form impressions based on appearance. You want to come across as respectful, responsible, and prepared.

Keep It Functional

You might be there for hours—wear layers in case it's hot or cold, and shoes you can stand or walk in comfortably.

Bring a professional-looking bag or folder for your documents—something neat and organized, not stuffed or chaotic.

If You're a Parent...

If custody is part of the hearing, dressing neatly can subtly reinforce that you're a stable, reliable caregiver.

Avoid bringing your children unless the court has asked you to—but if they must come, dress them neatly too.

Quick Tips:

- Iron your clothes.

- Avoid loud patterns.

- No hats or sunglasses indoors.

- Don't wear your wedding ring unless you have a reason to.

Find the Experts you need at freshstartsregistry.com/experts

Do I Need Legal Representation in Court?

While some people choose to represent themselves in court, having legal representation can make a significant difference. An attorney can help you understand court procedures, file the right paperwork, and advocate for your best interests. Even if you are handling much of the process on your own, consulting with an attorney before going to court can be a valuable safeguard.

Questions to Ask: Is it realistic for me to represent myself in court? What are the potential risks of not having a lawyer? Can I consult with an attorney just for the court appearance?

Action Step: If you're considering self-representation, attend a few court sessions to understand the expectations and procedures. If you feel uncertain, schedule a consultation with a lawyer who can advise you on how to prepare.

What If We Can't Agree on Key Issues?

Disagreements over custody, property, and financial support are common in divorce. If you and your spouse cannot come to an agreement, the court will intervene to make those decisions for you. This is known as a contested divorce and typically involves multiple court hearings and legal negotiations.

Questions to Ask: What happens if we can't agree on child custody or property division? How does the judge make decisions if we are in disagreement? Are there ways to resolve disputes without going to court?

Action Step: Consider mediation or collaborative divorce as a way to resolve conflicts before going to court. If those options don't work, prepare yourself with the documentation and evidence needed to present your case clearly and confidently.

Moving Forward

Understanding the legal process and what to expect during court appearances can significantly reduce the stress and uncertainty that often accompany divorce. By knowing the steps, preparing your documents, and familiarizing yourself with the courtroom environment, you take back control of your own experience. Whether you have legal representation or are navigating the process on your own, knowledge is your greatest ally.

CHAPTER 8

Everything You Need to Know About Postnuptial Agreements

When people think of marriage and legal agreements, prenuptial agreements often come to mind. But what happens if you're already married and want to protect your assets or establish financial boundaries? That's where a postnuptial agreement comes in. A postnuptial agreement is a legal contract created after marriage that outlines how assets, debts, and financial responsibilities will be handled in the event of a divorce. Understanding the purpose and benefits of a postnuptial agreement can help you decide if it's the right choice for your situation.

What is a Postnuptial Agreement?

A postnuptial agreement is similar to a prenuptial agreement, but it's created after the marriage has already taken place. It sets the terms for asset division, debt responsibility, and spousal support if the marriage ends. Unlike prenuptial agreements, which are often planned before any conflict arises, postnuptial agreements are sometimes prompted by financial changes, new business ventures, or relationship challenges.

Questions to Ask: What are the main reasons couples create postnuptial agreements? How does a postnuptial agreement differ from a prenuptial agreement? Can it be modified after it is signed?

Action Step: If you're considering a postnuptial agreement, begin by identifying the assets and financial responsibilities you want to protect. Have an open and honest conversation with your spouse about why you feel this agreement is necessary.

Why Would I Need a Postnuptial Agreement?

There are many reasons why a couple might decide to create a postnuptial agreement. Sometimes, one partner may inherit a significant amount of money or take on substantial business investments. Other times, financial disagreements or infidelity may prompt a desire to outline specific financial protections. Understanding your motivations can help you frame the conversation with your spouse and work towards mutual understanding.

Questions to Ask: Has there been a significant financial change in our marriage? Are we experiencing financial disagreements that need clarity? Would a postnuptial agreement help us feel more secure?

Action Step: Reflect on the reasons you want a postnuptial agreement. Write down your primary concerns—whether it's protecting an inheritance, clarifying debt responsibility, or safeguarding business assets. This will help you clearly communicate your intentions.

How Do You Create a Postnuptial Agreement?

The process of creating a postnuptial agreement typically involves both parties agreeing to the terms, consulting with separate attorneys, and signing the agreement in front of witnesses. It's crucial that both parties enter into the agreement willingly and fully informed, or it could be challenged in court later.

Questions to Ask: Do both partners need separate attorneys for a postnuptial agreement? What steps are involved in creating a legally binding agreement? How long does it take to complete the process?

Action Step: If you decide to move forward, research family law attorneys in your area who specialize in postnuptial agreements. Schedule consultations to understand their process and fees, and make sure both you and your spouse are comfortable with the chosen legal representation.

Are Postnuptial Agreements Enforceable?

Not all postnuptial agreements hold up in court. For the agreement to be enforceable, it must be fair, voluntarily signed by both parties, and executed with full financial disclosure. Courts may invalidate agreements that appear to be coerced, signed under duress, or are blatantly one-sided.

Questions to Ask: What factors make a postnuptial agreement enforceable? Can it be challenged in court, and under what circumstances? How often should it be updated or reviewed?

Action Step: Ensure that both you and your spouse fully understand the terms of the agreement and that it is written clearly and fairly. Consider having it reviewed by legal professionals to guarantee its strength and enforceability.

Moving Forward

A postnuptial agreement can provide clarity and security if financial changes or concerns arise during marriage. Understanding how to create one, why you might need it, and how to make it enforceable will help you make empowered decisions. If you believe that establishing these boundaries could benefit your situation, take the first step by starting the conversation and seeking legal guidance.

CHAPTER 9

Real Estate, Estate Planning, and Assets

When you start thinking about ending a marriage, the emotional weight is just one part of the story—there's also a whole layer of practical decisions to face. Things like what to do with the house, how to divide up your savings, and whether your estate plan needs a refresh. These aren't just documents and numbers—they're tied to the life you built together. It can feel like a lot, but understanding how your home, your money, and your plans for the future might be impacted is a powerful first step.

In this chapter, we'll walk you through the key areas: real estate, estate planning, and shared assets. We know it can be overwhelming, especially when emotions are high and everything feels uncertain—but you don't have to go into this blind. With a little guidance and the right questions, you can start making choices that protect your future and give you a sense of control.

You don't have to do this alone. We're here to guide you through it, one step at a time.

4 Essential Real Estate Considerations for Those Contemplating Divorce

1. Understand Property Ownership and Equity

What It Is: Determine how your property is owned (e.g., jointly or individually) and assess the equity you have in it. Equity is the difference between the property's market value and the amount owed on the mortgage.

Why It's Important: This will help you understand the financial implications of keeping or selling the property, and it's crucial for dividing assets fairly.

Who Can Help: A real estate attorney or a financial advisor specializing in divorce.

How to Ask for Help: Contact a real estate attorney and say: "I'm considering divorce and need help understanding the ownership structure of my home and the implications for asset division. Can you guide me through this?"

Ask questions like: "What does joint ownership mean in a divorce? How can I determine my home's current equity?"

2. Evaluate Affordability Post-Divorce

What It Is: Analyze whether you or your spouse can afford to keep the property on a single income, including mortgage payments, taxes, insurance, and maintenance costs.

Why It's Important: Ensuring financial stability post-divorce is crucial, and keeping a home that is unaffordable can lead to long-term financial strain.

Who Can Help: A mortgage lender or financial planner with expertise in divorce scenarios.

How to Ask for Help: Reach out to a mortgage lender and say: "I'm evaluating the financial feasibility of keeping my home after a potential divorce. Can you provide an assessment of my options?"

Ask questions like: "What would my refinancing options look like on my current income? What costs should I anticipate if I keep the property?"

3. Consider Market Value and Timing

What It Is: Assess the current market value of your home and determine whether it's a good time to sell based on market conditions.

Why It's Important: Selling the home may be necessary to divide assets, and understanding market conditions can maximize financial outcomes.

Who Can Help: A real estate agent or appraiser.

How to Ask for Help: Consult a real estate agent and say: "I'm considering divorce and need to understand my home's market value and the best timing for a potential sale. Can you provide insights?"

Ask questions like: "What is my home currently worth? How long does it typically take to sell a property in this market?"

4. Explore the Emotional Impact of Selling or Keeping the Home

What It Is: Reflect on how keeping or selling the home will affect you and your family emotionally. The family home often carries sentimental value and represents stability.

Why It's Important: Divorce is a major emotional transition, and making a clear decision about the home can help ease the adjustment for you and your family.

Who Can Help: A therapist or divorce coach.

How to Ask for Help: Talk to a therapist and say: "I'm considering divorce and need guidance on processing the emotional aspects of potentially selling my home."

Ask questions like: "How can I weigh the emotional attachment to my home against the financial and practical considerations? How can I prepare myself and my children for a potential move?"

4 Essential Considerations for Your Estate Planning If You're Considering Divorce

1. Review Your Beneficiary Designations

What It Is: Examine who is listed as a beneficiary on your life insurance policies, retirement accounts, and other financial instruments.

Why It's Important: Divorce doesn't automatically change these designations, and your spouse may still be entitled to these assets if they remain listed.

Who Can Help: An estate planning attorney or financial advisor.

How to Ask for Help: Reach out to an estate planning attorney and say: "I'm considering divorce and need help reviewing my beneficiary designations to ensure they reflect my current intentions."

"Which accounts and policies should I update, and what's the process for changing beneficiaries?"

2. Update or Create a Will

What It Is: Ensure your will reflects your wishes regarding asset distribution and guardianship (if applicable).

Why It's Important: A will created during marriage often includes your spouse as a primary beneficiary or executor, which may no longer align with your goals.

Who Can Help: An estate planning attorney.

How to Ask for Help: Consult an attorney and say: "I'm planning for a possible divorce and want to ensure my will reflects my current wishes. Can you guide me through revising or creating one?"

Ask questions like: "What changes should I make to my will during this process? How do I name a new executor or guardian?"

3. Establish Powers of Attorney

What It Is: Update your financial and medical powers of attorney, which designate who will make decisions on your behalf if you're unable to do so.

Why It's Important: If your spouse is currently listed, you may want to designate someone else to act in these roles during and after divorce.

Who Can Help: An estate planning attorney.

How to Ask for Help: Engage an attorney and say: "I'm considering divorce and want to update my financial and medical powers of attorney to reflect a different decision-maker."

Ask questions like: "How do I choose a new power of attorney, and what steps are involved in updating these documents?"

4. Assess Trusts or Joint Accounts

What It Is: Evaluate any trusts or joint financial accounts you've established with your spouse, including family trusts or joint investment accounts.

Why It's Important: These accounts may need to be restructured or dissolved to align with your post-divorce financial plan.

Who Can Help: A trust attorney or financial advisor.

How to Ask for Help: Speak to a trust attorney and say: "I'm preparing for a possible divorce and need to review any trusts or joint accounts I have with my spouse to understand my options."

Ask questions like: "What happens to shared trusts or accounts in a divorce? How can I ensure my interests are protected in these arrangements?"

4 Essential Considerations for Your Assets If You're Considering Divorce

1. Inventory All Assets

What It Is: Create a detailed list of all assets you and your spouse own, including bank accounts, investments, properties, vehicles, and personal items of significant value.

Why It's Important: Understanding the full scope of your shared and individual assets is critical for equitable division and helps you protect your financial interests.

Who Can Help: A financial advisor or forensic accountant.

How to Ask for Help: Reach out to a financial advisor and say: "I'm considering divorce and need help creating a complete inventory of our assets."

Ask questions like: "What tools or methods can I use to ensure I've accounted for everything? How do I identify hidden or overlooked assets?"

ASSET INVENTORY

ASSET	*DESCRIPTION*	*CATEGORY*	*VALUE*

Date: _____   **Page**_____ **of**_____

2. Determine Asset Classification: Marital vs. Separate

What It Is: Distinguish between marital assets (acquired during the marriage) and separate assets (owned before marriage or received as gifts/inheritance).

Why It's Important: Only marital assets are typically subject to division during divorce, so proper classification protects your separate property.

Who Can Help: A divorce attorney or financial expert.

How to Ask for Help: Consult a divorce attorney and say: "I'd like to understand which assets may be classified as marital or separate as I prepare for divorce."

Ask questions like: "How can I provide proof of ownership for my separate assets? What records or documents are required to support my claims?"

3. Evaluate Debt Responsibilities

What It Is: Assess any joint or individual debts, such as mortgages, credit card balances, student loans, or car loans, and understand who is responsible for each.

Why It's Important: Debt is divided alongside assets in divorce, so knowing your liabilities helps you prepare for potential outcomes and avoid surprises.

Who Can Help: A financial advisor or credit counselor.

How to Ask for Help: Contact a financial advisor and say: "I'm preparing for a potential divorce and need a clear picture of our shared and individual debts."

Ask questions like: "How will debt division work in a divorce? What steps can I take to protect myself from being held liable for my spouse's debts?"

4. Assess Tax Implications

What It Is: Understand how dividing or selling assets during divorce could impact your tax obligations, such as capital gains taxes, property transfers, or retirement account penalties.

Why It's Important: Proper planning can help you minimize financial losses and avoid unexpected tax bills.

Who Can Help: A tax advisor or CPA with experience in divorce.

How to Ask for Help: Approach a tax advisor and say: "I'm considering divorce and want to understand how asset division might affect my tax obligations."

Ask questions like: "What tax implications should I consider for selling or transferring assets? How can I prepare for these during the divorce process?"

CHAPTER 10

Financial Considerations, Banking, Credit Cards, And Debt

Divorce can be an emotionally charged and overwhelming experience, but one of the most practical aspects to address early on is your finances. Whether you've been together for a few years or many, understanding how divorce will impact your financial future is crucial. From untangling joint bank accounts to determining how debt will be divided, there's a lot to consider. In this post, we'll explore key financial considerations, including banking, debt, and personal financial planning, to help you navigate this challenging time with clarity and confidence. Divorce isn't just an emotional experience—it's also a financial one. Whether you've been married for a few years or a few decades, the process of untangling your financial life from your partner's can feel daunting. But understanding where you stand financially is one of the most empowering steps you can take. Knowledge is power, and as you begin to consider the path forward, having a clear picture of your financial landscape can make all the difference.

In many marriages, finances are deeply intertwined. There are joint bank accounts, shared credit cards, mortgage payments, and possibly even business ventures that link your financial well-being to your partner's. Before you can even begin to understand what divorce might look like for you, it's crucial to have a solid grasp of your financial situation. This includes understanding what you owe, what you own, and how your money moves in and out of your accounts each month.

Banking is often one of the first practical considerations during the contemplation stage. Knowing what accounts you have, who has access to them, and how funds are being managed is vital. This is also the time to start thinking about whether it's appropriate to open a separate account to protect your individual finances during the process.

Credit cards are another significant area of focus. Shared credit card debt is common, but what many people don't realize is that the credit card company doesn't care who racked up the charges—they just want their money back. Understanding how credit card debt is divided in divorce and knowing what steps you can take to protect your credit score is essential.

And then there's debt. Mortgages, car loans, student loans, and other debts can become complicated during divorce proceedings. It's not just about knowing what you owe, but understanding how that debt is tied to both of your names—and how it might be divided.

In this chapter, we'll guide you through these critical financial considerations. We'll help you create a clear financial picture, understand your rights, and prepare you to make informed decisions that will protect your financial stability during and after divorce.

You don't have to navigate this alone. We're here to help you face these financial realities with clarity and strength.

4 Essential Financial Considerations When Considering Divorce

1. Understand Your Current Financial Situation

What It Is: Before initiating the divorce process, it's crucial to get a clear picture of your current finances—assets, liabilities, income, and expenses.

Why It's Important: Knowing your financial standing will help you make informed decisions moving forward and avoid surprises. It's vital for preparing for negotiations and understanding what you might be entitled to in terms of alimony or division of assets.

Experts Who Can Help: A financial planner or a Certified Divorce Financial Analyst (CDFA) can help you assess your financial situation.

How to Ask for Help: Reach out to a financial professional with a question like, "Can you help me understand my financial picture and prepare for a potential divorce? I'd like to be fully informed on my assets and liabilities before moving forward."

2. Review Joint Bank Accounts and Credit

What It Is: Identify and review all joint bank accounts, credit cards, and loans that you share with your spouse.

Why It's Important: Understanding the state of your joint financial obligations is essential for protecting your credit and ensuring you aren't caught off guard by any financial surprises. In many cases, it's a good idea to open individual accounts to separate your finances before making the divorce official.

Experts Who Can Help: A financial advisor or a credit counselor can provide guidance on how to navigate and protect your credit during this transition.

How to Ask for Help: Contact a financial advisor and ask, "Can you help me set up separate accounts and review my credit situation to make sure I'm prepared for financial independence?"

3. Plan for Division of Debt and Assets

What It Is: Understand how debt and assets might be divided in the event of a divorce. This includes property, savings, retirement accounts, and any joint debts

Why It's Important: Knowing how your debts and assets will be divided helps you anticipate your future financial responsibilities and plan accordingly. It's important to have a clear understanding before entering negotiations or legal proceedings.

Experts Who Can Help: A divorce attorney and a Certified Divorce Financial Analyst (CDFA) can offer insight into how assets and debts are typically divided in your state.

How to Ask for Help: Approach a CDFA and ask, "Can you help me understand how my assets and debts might be divided in a divorce, and what steps I can take to protect my financial interests?"

4. Consider Long-Term Financial Planning

What It Is: Think about your financial future beyond the immediate aftermath of divorce, including retirement plans, health insurance, and future savings.

Why It's Important: Divorce can significantly impact long-term financial goals, so it's crucial to start planning for the future—especially when it comes to retirement and any health-related expenses. This will help you adjust to your new reality and ensure financial stability.

Experts Who Can Help: A financial planner or retirement specialist can guide you in adjusting your long-term goals.

How to Ask for Help: Ask a financial planner, "Can you help me reassess my retirement and financial goals in light of the potential divorce? I want to ensure I'm financially prepared for the future."

4 Essential Debt and Credit Considerations When Considering Divorce

1. Review Joint Debt and Financial Obligations

What It Is: Take an inventory of any debts you and your spouse share, including credit card balances, personal loans, mortgages, and auto loans.

Why It's Important: Understanding who is legally responsible for joint debt after the divorce is crucial. If debts are not properly addressed, you may remain responsible for obligations even after the divorce is finalized.

Experts Who Can Help: A financial advisor or a Certified Divorce Financial Analyst (CDFA) can help you assess shared debt and create a strategy for handling it.

How to Ask for Help: Reach out to a financial professional and say, "Can you help me review all of our joint debts and figure out how they should be divided or handled before divorce proceedings?"

2. Understand How Divorce Affects Your Credit

What It Is: Your credit score may be impacted by divorce, especially if there is shared debt or if you rely on joint accounts that could be left unsettled.

Why It's Important: Divorce can cause changes in creditworthiness, so it's essential to separate your credit profile early on to avoid negative effects from joint financial obligations.

Experts Who Can Help: A credit counselor or financial advisor can offer advice on how to protect your credit during the divorce process.

How to Ask for Help: Contact a credit counselor and ask, "Can you help me understand how divorce will impact my credit and what steps I can take to safeguard my credit score moving forward?"

3. Separate Joint Accounts and Credit Cards

What It Is: Take steps to open individual accounts and remove yourself from joint credit cards or lines of credit.

Why It's Important: Keeping joint accounts open during divorce can lead to financial complications, especially if your spouse continues to use them. It's vital to establish financial independence early on.

Experts Who Can Help: A financial advisor or an attorney can guide you through the process of separating finances.

How to Ask for Help: Ask a financial advisor, "Can you help me separate our joint accounts and ensure my name is removed from any credit cards or loans that are still shared?"

4. Plan for Dividing Debt in the Divorce Settlement

What It Is: Understand how debt division will be handled in the divorce settlement, including who will be responsible for certain debts and how they'll be paid off.

Why It's Important: How debt is divided can significantly impact your financial future. A fair division of debt is crucial to avoid ongoing financial strain and ensure you're not left with more than your fair share.

Experts Who Can Help: A divorce attorney and a Certified Divorce Financial Analyst (CDFA) can help you understand your rights and negotiate the division of debt during the divorce process.

How to Ask for Help: Reach out to your attorney or a CDFA and say, "Can you explain how debt is typically divided in a divorce and help me make sure the settlement is fair and manageable?"

4 Essential Personal Finance and Banking Considerations When Considering Divorce

1. Assess Your Joint Bank Accounts and Separate Accounts

What It Is: Review all joint bank accounts, credit cards, and financial accounts shared with your spouse. Consider how to separate these accounts before initiating the divorce process.

Why It's Important: Keeping joint accounts open during divorce can lead to complications, especially if your spouse continues to withdraw money or rack up charges. Separating finances early helps you maintain control over your financial assets.

Find the Experts you need at freshstartsregistry.com/experts

Why It's Important: Keeping joint accounts open during divorce can lead to complications, especially if your spouse continues to withdraw money or rack up charges. Separating finances early helps you maintain control over your financial assets.

Experts Who Can Help: A financial advisor or a Certified Divorce Financial Analyst (CDFA) can help you create a strategy for separating your accounts.

How to Ask for Help: Contact a financial expert and say, "Can you help me separate our joint accounts and set up my own personal banking system before the divorce process starts?"

2. Understand the Impact of Divorce on Your Credit Score

What It Is: Divorce can impact your credit score, especially if there is shared debt or if you fail to separate your financial obligations properly.

Why It's Important: It's important to protect your credit score and prevent your spouse from making decisions that could affect your financial standing. Early planning can help you avoid negative financial consequences.

Experts Who Can Help: A credit counselor or financial advisor can offer advice on safeguarding your credit during and after divorce.

How to Ask for Help: Ask a credit counselor, "Can you help me understand how my credit may be affected by the divorce, and what steps I can take to protect my credit score?"

3. Create a Personal Financial Plan for Life After Divorce

What It Is: Develop a financial plan for your life post-divorce, including budgeting for new living arrangements, child support or alimony, and any adjustments to your lifestyle.

Why It's Important: Understanding your financial needs post-divorce ensures you're not left financially unprepared for the changes ahead. A solid financial plan can help you create stability and clarity for your future.

Experts Who Can Help: A financial planner or Certified Divorce Financial Analyst (CDFA) can help you create a comprehensive financial plan that accounts for post-divorce expenses.

How to Ask for Help: Approach a financial planner and say, "Can you help me create a budget and financial plan for my life after divorce? I want to make sure I'm financially stable and ready for the future."

4. Understand How Divorce Affects Retirement Accounts and Investments

What It Is: Review how your retirement savings, investment accounts, and other assets will be divided in the divorce. Understand the potential impact on your long-term financial security.

Why It's Important: Divorce can significantly affect your retirement savings, and it's essential to know how your investments and retirement accounts will be divided to plan for the future. Ensuring an equitable division of assets can protect your financial future.

Experts Who Can Help: A Certified Divorce Financial Analyst (CDFA) or financial advisor can guide you in understanding how your retirement assets will be divided.

How to Ask for Help: Contact a CDFA and ask, "Can you help me understand how my retirement savings and investments will be divided in the divorce, and how I can ensure I'm financially secure moving forward?"

By addressing these essential financial considerations early, you can take proactive steps to protect your financial health and make informed decisions during the divorce process. Reaching out to the right experts will ensure you're on the right path to a stable financial future.

CHAPTER 11

—————

Navigating Social Security and Retirement Benefits

When you're considering divorce, it's easy to focus on immediate concerns—custody, housing, bank accounts. But your long-term financial stability matters just as much. One often overlooked but essential area to explore is how divorce will impact your Social Security benefits and retirement accounts. These assets can significantly affect your financial future, especially if you've been out of the workforce or earned less during the marriage.

Understanding what you're entitled to and how to protect your long-term income is key. In this chapter, we'll walk you through the questions to ask, why they matter, and how to take action now to secure your future.

Am I Eligible to Claim Social Security Based on My Spouse's Record?

If you were married for at least ten years, you may be eligible to receive Social Security benefits based on your ex-spouse's earnings record. This can be especially helpful if you earned significantly less or were a stay-at-home parent during the marriage. It doesn't reduce your ex-spouse's benefits and you don't need to inform them to apply.

Questions to Ask: Were we married for at least ten consecutive years? Am I at least 62 years old or nearing retirement age? Is my own Social Security benefit lower than what I'd receive from my ex-spouse's record?

Action Step: Contact the Social Security Administration to learn more about your eligibility. Bring your marriage certificate and divorce decree, and ask for a benefits estimate based on your ex-spouse's record.

How Will Our Retirement Accounts Be Divided?

Retirement savings, such as 401(k)s, IRAs, and pensions, are often among the largest marital assets. In many states, these are subject to division in divorce, even if only one spouse contributed to the account. Understanding how these accounts are valued and divided is essential for planning your post-divorce financial life.

Questions to Ask: What retirement accounts exist under either of our names? How are these accounts treated in divorce under state law? Will I need a Qualified Domestic Relations Order (QDRO) to access a portion of these funds?

Action Step: Make a list of all retirement accounts and request the most recent statements. Meet with a financial advisor or attorney to understand how these funds may be divided and whether you need a QDRO to receive your portion without penalties.

What Happens to Pension Plans or Government Benefits?

If your spouse has a pension or is entitled to government retirement benefits (such as military or federal employee retirement plans), you may have a legal claim to a portion of those benefits. These plans often have their own set of rules for division and may require additional paperwork.

Questions to Ask: Does my spouse have a pension or government retirement plan? Am I entitled to a share of those benefits? What steps do I need to take to ensure I receive my portion?

Action Step: Request plan documentation from your spouse or their employer. Work with an attorney who has experience with dividing pensions and government benefits to ensure nothing is overlooked.

How Can I Protect My Retirement if I Was Not the Primary Earner?

If you didn't contribute as much to retirement savings during your marriage, it's important to advocate for your fair share. This includes negotiating for a portion of retirement accounts or considering spousal support to help you rebuild retirement savings post-divorce.

Questions to Ask: What will my financial picture look like in retirement after divorce? How can I start rebuilding my own retirement savings? Should I negotiate for additional support to make up for lost savings?

Action Step: Meet with a financial planner to create a post-divorce retirement strategy. Consider contributing to an IRA in your own name or increasing savings if you're working again. Look into catch-up contributions if you're over 50.

Moving Forward

Navigating Social Security and retirement benefits during divorce can feel overwhelming, but these steps are crucial to ensuring long-term financial security. By asking the right questions now and working with professionals who understand these systems, you can protect your future and step into the next chapter with confidence and clarity.

CHAPTER 12

—

Digital Assets and
Online Security

In the digital age, your online presence is just as important as your physical assets—especially during a divorce. From shared streaming accounts to bank logins, photo storage, and even social media, our digital lives are deeply intertwined with our relationships. Divorce isn't just about dividing homes and bank accounts anymore; it also means protecting your online identity and regaining control over your digital world.

This chapter will help you think through your digital footprint, ask the right questions, and take steps to protect your personal information, privacy, and security as you begin your next chapter.

What Online Accounts Are Connected to Both of Us?

Start by asking yourself which digital accounts are shared or jointly accessed. This could include everything from bank and credit card accounts to Netflix, Amazon, and iCloud. Identifying what's shared helps you understand what needs to be separated or closed, and what might still be vulnerable.

Questions to Ask: Which logins or services do we both have access to? Do any shared accounts contain personal data, financial info, or stored files? Are there any auto-payments or subscriptions tied to shared accounts?

Action Step: Make a list of all shared digital accounts. Go through your phone, computer, browser bookmarks, and email inbox for reminders. Start the process of creating new accounts in your own name and update logins, passwords, and recovery methods for anything you want to keep.

———

Digital Accounts Separation Worksheet

Step 1: List Shared Digital Accounts

Go through your phone, computer, browser bookmarks, and inbox to identify shared or connected accounts. Use the table to track what needs to be updated, closed, or separated.

Find the Experts you need at freshstartsregistry.com/experts

Digital Accounts Separation Worksheet

Account/Platform	Type (Streaming, Banking, Email)	Shared With?	Action Needed (Keep, Close, Separate)	New Account Created? (Y/N)	Notes

Digital Accounts Separation Worksheet

Account/ Platform	Type (Streaming, Banking, Email)	Shared With?	Action Needed (Keep, Close, Separate)	New Account Created? (Y/N)	Notes

Digital Accounts Separation Checklist

Step 2: Update Your Info

Use this checklist to make sure you're updating your personal access and security settings:

☐ Create new email address (if needed)

☐ Update passwords for accounts you'll keep

☐ Change recovery email and phone number

☐ Enable two-factor authentication

☐ Remove ex-partner from shared logins/devices

☐ Export or save anything you want to keep (photos, files, subscriptions, etc.)

Tips:

- If you're unsure whether you're listed on an account, check your inbox for sign-up or billing emails.

- Don't forget subscriptions tucked inside Apple ID, Google Play, or Amazon accounts.

- Keep a secure master list of your new logins in a password manager or locked document.

Do I Need to Change My Passwords and Email Logins?

Protecting your online identity is crucial. If your spouse knows your passwords—or has access to your email—they may be able to see sensitive information, even unintentionally. Password updates are an essential part of establishing privacy and maintaining digital boundaries.

Questions to Ask: Does my spouse have access to any of my current logins or devices? Have I reused the same passwords across multiple platforms? Is my email secure and private?

Action Step: Create new, strong passwords for your personal email and any accounts you use independently. Use a password manager to safely store new login information. Enable two-factor authentication (2FA) wherever possible to add an extra layer of protection.

What Should I Do About Shared Devices and Cloud Storage?

Laptops, tablets, phones, and cloud storage accounts often contain years of photos, documents, and browser histories. If you've shared devices or backed up your data to shared iCloud or Google accounts, it's time to regain ownership of your digital life.

Questions to Ask: Are there shared devices that still have my personal accounts logged in? Is my data backed up to a cloud account my spouse can access? What digital content (photos, videos, documents) do I want to save or protect?

Action Step: Log out of any devices your spouse might have access to. Transfer or download copies of personal photos, messages, or documents you want to keep. Create new backups linked to your personal email and accounts.

Am I Digitally Safe from Tracking or Monitoring?

While most divorces are respectful, it's still wise to consider your digital safety. Some spouses may use tracking apps or shared location services, sometimes unknowingly. Taking back your privacy is not about paranoia—it's about personal empowerment.

Questions to Ask: Is my phone or laptop connected to a shared Apple ID, Google account, or family tracking plan? Could my location be visible to my spouse through apps like Find My iPhone or Life360? Have I checked my devices for any unfamiliar apps or software?

Action Step: Turn off location sharing features. Review settings in apps like Find My, Google Maps, and messaging services. If needed, do a factory reset on devices you feel unsure about and reconnect them using new accounts.

Moving Forward

Digital security may not be the first thing you think about when considering divorce, but it's one of the most critical components of protecting your future. By asking yourself these questions and taking action to safeguard your accounts and devices, you reclaim control over your information and build a secure foundation for your next chapter.

CHAPTER 13

Protecting Your Privacy and Setting Boundaries

People talk a lot about how divorce changes your legal status or your emotional world—but it also changes your social landscape in big ways. Suddenly, folks who never asked about your relationship before might feel entitled to the play-by-play. Friends might pick sides. Family might offer unsolicited advice. Even coworkers and acquaintances can start acting… weird.

That's why setting boundaries and protecting your privacy isn't just helpful—it's necessary. You get to decide what you share, who you share it with, and how you want to be supported. In this chapter, we'll help you get clear on your boundaries, prepare for tough conversations, and figure out how to protect your peace as your world shifts around you.

What Information Am I Comfortable Sharing—and With Whom?

You don't owe anyone your story. Not everyone needs to know the details of your separation, and it's okay to be selective about who you confide in. Being clear about what you want to share—and with whom—can help you maintain a sense of control when so much may feel uncertain.

Questions to Ask: Who do I trust with personal details about my divorce? What feels safe and respectful for me to share? Are there certain topics that are off-limits for discussion?

Action Step: Choose a short, neutral phrase you can use when someone asks a question you don't want to answer—something like, "I'm keeping things private right now but appreciate your support." Having this ready will make setting boundaries easier in the moment.

How Do I Handle Social Media During Divorce?

Social media can amplify stress during divorce. What you post (or don't post) might be interpreted in ways you don't intend. If your spouse, their friends, or extended family follow you, it may feel like your life is on display. Taking a thoughtful approach to your digital presence helps you protect your emotional and legal well-being.

Questions to Ask: Who can see what I post online? Am I using social media to express myself or to seek validation? Would I be okay with a judge or my children seeing this post someday?

Action Step: Review your social media privacy settings. Consider taking a break or limiting your activity online. Use private journals or trusted confidants for emotional processing instead of public posts.

What Boundaries Do I Need with My Ex?

Whether you're still under the same roof or already living apart, boundaries with your ex are vital. These boundaries can be emotional, physical, digital, or conversational—and they help create the space you need to heal and think clearly.

Questions to Ask: What topics feel too triggering or personal to discuss right now? What forms of communication are healthiest for us during this transition? Are there times or places where I need space?

Action Step: Identify one boundary that would help you feel more stable this week—such as only communicating through email or taking a break from shared social plans. Communicate that boundary clearly, and hold it gently but firmly.

How Do I Manage Outside Opinions and Unsolicited Advice?

During divorce, you may find yourself fielding unsolicited opinions from well-meaning people who want to help—or just want to gossip. It's okay to say no to these conversations. You get to decide who gets access to your story and energy.

Questions to Ask: Are the people offering advice actually supportive of me, or are they projecting their own experience? How do I feel after talking to this person—more clear or more confused? Do I want to continue this conversation, or do I need to redirect or pause it?

Action Step: Practice phrases that shut down unwanted input with kindness. Try, "I appreciate your concern, but I'm working through this in my own way," or "I'm not looking for advice right now—just support." Repeat as needed.

Moving Forward

Setting boundaries and protecting your privacy is not about being secretive or cold—it's about creating space to heal, think, and rebuild. The clearer you are about what you're willing to share and with whom, the more empowered you'll feel during this vulnerable time. Boundaries are how you honor your energy, and privacy is how you protect your peace

———

CHAPTER 14

Deciding Whether to Keep or Sell the Family Home

The family home often holds more than just furniture and walls—it carries memories, routines, comfort, and identity. That's what makes the decision to keep or sell it during divorce so emotionally and financially charged. Whether it's a place you raised your kids, a house you built together, or simply the space where your daily life unfolded, deciding what to do with your home is one of the biggest considerations in the divorce process.

This chapter will help you ask the right questions about your home, understand what's at stake, and take informed steps toward a decision that aligns with your emotional well-being and financial future.

What Does the Home Represent to Me?

Start by tuning into your emotional connection to the home. Ask yourself what the space means to you, and whether holding onto it is about comfort—or something else. Sometimes the desire to stay is rooted in stability or a fear of change. Other times, it's a symbolic choice about reclaiming space. There's no wrong answer—but there are honest ones.

Questions to Ask: Am I attached to this house because it feels safe, or because I'm afraid of starting over? Does this home bring me peace—or does it hold painful memories? Am I willing to take on the full responsibility of this space emotionally and financially?

Action Step: Journal about what the home means to you. Write down what you love about it, what feels hard, and what you fear about leaving. Clarity begins when you acknowledge what's beneath the surface.

Can I Afford to Keep the Home on My Own?

It's easy to become emotionally attached to the idea of staying—but it's crucial to assess whether you can realistically afford it. This includes not just the mortgage, but also taxes, maintenance, insurance, and utilities. Keeping the home can be empowering, but only if it's financially sustainable.

Questions to Ask: What are the full monthly costs of owning this home? Do I qualify to refinance the mortgage in my name alone? Would staying in this house prevent me from reaching other financial goals?

Action Step: Create a detailed monthly budget with all home-related expenses. If possible, meet with a mortgage lender to explore refinancing options. Then compare the numbers to your projected post-divorce income.

Home Budget & Refinance Planning Worksheet

Step 1: List All Monthly Home-Related Expenses

Expense Category	Monthly Amount	Notes (due date, split/shared, variable?)
Mortgage/Rent		
Property Taxes		
Homeowners Insurance		
Utilities (electric, gas)		
Water/Sewer		
Internet/Cable		
Maintenance/ Repairs		
Lawn/Snow Services		
HOA Fees (if applicable)		
Security System		
Other		
Other		
TOTAL Monthly Expenses		

Home Budget & Refinance Planning Worksheet

Step 2: Mortgage & Refinance Exploration

☐ Have I spoken with a mortgage lender?

☐ Can I qualify to refinance the mortgage solo?

☐ What would the new monthly payment be?

☐ What closing costs or fees would apply?

☐ Do I need to buy out my ex's share of equity?

☐ What's the current value of the home?

Step 3: Compare to Your Post-Divorce Income

Monthly Net Income (after taxes)

	Amount
Estimated Income from Work	
Child Support / Alimony	
Other Income (side gigs, etc.)	
TOTAL Monthly Income	

Can you afford to stay in the home based on your income and projected home expenses?

☐ Yes ☐ No ☐ Not sure yet — need more info

Next Steps:

- Talk to a mortgage lender or financial advisor

- Explore your post-divorce budget as a whole

- Get an updated appraisal on the home (if needed)

- Reflect on what "home" means to you moving forward

Find the Experts you need at freshstartsregistry.com/experts

What Would Selling the Home Mean for My Next Chapter?

Sometimes, selling the home can create a fresh start. It can allow for a financial reset, an emotional release, and the chance to build a life on your own terms. If you're feeling torn, it may help to imagine the freedom that comes with letting go.

Questions to Ask: Would selling the home give me more flexibility and financial breathing room? Am I open to the possibility that a new space could feel more like mine? Could the sale of the home help fund my transition into post-divorce life?

Action Step: Visualize what a new home or living situation might look like. Write down what you'd want in a new space—quiet, light, safety, affordability—and how it might better serve the person you're becoming.

What Are the Legal and Logistical Steps Involved?

Whether you keep or sell the home, there are legal and logistical steps that need to be handled properly. You'll need to decide how equity will be divided, who pays for what in the interim, and how the title or mortgage will be handled going forward.

Questions to Ask: How will the home's value and equity be calculated and divided? Who will cover the mortgage and upkeep during the divorce process? What paperwork is needed to transfer ownership or complete the sale?

Action Step: Meet with your attorney and a real estate professional to understand your legal rights, equity position, and the process of either selling or refinancing. Knowing the exact steps will help make a difficult decision more manageable.

Moving Forward

Deciding what to do with the family home is one of the most emotional and practical choices you'll make during divorce. There's no one-size-fits-all answer. What matters is making a decision rooted in clarity, not fear. Whether you choose to stay and reclaim your space or sell and start fresh, know that you are capable of building a home that truly supports the life you want to live next.

CHAPTER 15

Everything to Know About Mediation

Mediation is one of the most empowering and collaborative ways to approach divorce. Rather than facing off in a courtroom, mediation allows couples to work with a neutral third-party professional to reach agreements together. This path is often less expensive, less adversarial, and more focused on mutual resolution than traditional litigation. But while mediation can be a powerful option, it's not right for everyone—and understanding what to expect is key.

In this chapter, we'll walk you through the basics of mediation, the questions to ask yourself before choosing this route, and the practical steps to get started if you decide it's the right fit.

What Is Mediation, and How Does It Work?

Mediation is a voluntary process where both parties work with a trained mediator to resolve divorce-related issues such as custody, property division, spousal support, and more. The mediator does not represent either party—they are there to facilitate a productive, respectful conversation and help guide you toward agreement.

Questions to Ask: What issues do we need to resolve during our divorce? Can we communicate respectfully enough to participate in joint sessions? Are we both open to compromise?

Action Step: Head to Fresh Starts Registry to find certified, vetted mediators who are professional, compassionate, and ready to support your next chapter. And don't forget to download our free e-book, 250+ Questions to Help You Build Your Divorce Support Team—it's packed with everything you need to feel prepared and empowered. Once you've started your search, research mediators in your area and look for those certified in divorce or family mediation. Before your first session, take a few minutes to jot down the key issues you'd like to address, so you can walk into the room ready to advocate for what matters most.

Is Mediation a Good Fit for Our Situation?

Mediation can be incredibly effective, but it does require that both parties are willing to engage in good faith. If there is a significant power imbalance, history of abuse, or deep mistrust, mediation might not be the best option. The success of mediation depends on both parties being committed to resolution rather than revenge.

Questions to Ask: Do I feel safe and heard in conversations with my spouse? Can I express my needs clearly in a shared setting? Is my spouse willing to compromise and collaborate?

Action Step: Reflect honestly on your communication dynamic. If you feel unsure, you can ask to meet with a mediator alone first to explore whether mediation feels like a safe and constructive path forward.

What Are the Benefits of Mediation?

Mediation tends to be less expensive and more efficient than court-based divorce. It also allows you to have more control over the outcome. Instead of leaving decisions up to a judge, you and your spouse create solutions that work for your unique family. Many people also find that mediation fosters a more peaceful co-parenting relationship.

Questions to Ask: Do I want more control over the outcome of my divorce? Am I looking for a process that prioritizes respect and dignity? Could mediation help preserve a healthier dynamic between us moving forward?

Action Step: Make a list of your priorities for the divorce process—whether it's protecting your kids from conflict, reducing costs, or feeling heard. Compare those goals to what mediation offers, and see if there's alignment.

What Should I Know Before We Begin?

Preparation is key to a successful mediation experience. You'll need to gather financial documents, understand your rights, and come ready to listen and speak honestly. While you don't need a lawyer present during mediation, it's often wise to consult with one beforehand so you understand what you're agreeing to.

Questions to Ask: Do I understand my financial and legal rights going into this process? What documents do I need to bring to mediation sessions? Should I consult a lawyer before I sign any final agreements?

Action Step: Create a folder of all relevant documents—bank statements, pay stubs, mortgage info, retirement accounts—and bring it to your first session. Schedule a consultation with a divorce attorney to review your rights and responsibilities in advance.

Moving Forward

Mediation can be a powerful and compassionate path through divorce. If you and your spouse are willing to work together, it can save time, money, and emotional strain. By understanding what mediation involves and preparing thoughtfully, you can move through this process with greater peace, clarity, and dignity.

CHAPTER 16

Everything to Do with Custody and Children

If you're considering divorce and have children, one of the most emotional and important parts of the process will be creating a custody arrangement that supports their well-being. This isn't just about legal rights—it's about routines, emotional safety, consistency, and long-term growth. Custody decisions will shape not just your relationship with your children, but also their sense of stability during a major life transition.

This chapter will help you understand the different types of custody, how decisions are made, and what steps you can take to advocate for your children's best interests with compassion and clarity.

What Types of Custody Exist, and What Might Work Best for Our Family?

Custody is typically broken down into two parts: legal custody (who makes major decisions for the child) and physical custody (where the child lives). Both can be joint or sole, and there's a wide range of possible arrangements based on what works best for each family. The right arrangement is the one that prioritizes your child's needs and fits your unique circumstances.

Questions to Ask: Do we want to share decision-making responsibilities, or does one parent need to take the lead? What kind of physical custody schedule would support our child's routine and stability? Are we able to collaborate respectfully when it comes to parenting decisions?

Action Step: Create a written list of your child's daily and weekly routines—school, bedtime, extracurriculars, meals, and healthcare needs. Use that as a foundation for thinking about what kind of custody schedule would be least disruptive and most nurturing.

Custody Planning & Routine Worksheet

Step 1: Map Out Your Child's Daily & Weekly Routines

Category	*Days of the Week/ Dates*	*Time*	*Location*	*People Involved/ Notes*
School Schedule				
Morning Routine				
After-School Routine				
Bedtime Routine				
Meals (dinner, snacks)				
Extracurriculars				
Weekend Activities				
Healthcare Appointments / Needs				

Custody Planning & Routine Worksheet

Step 2: Reflect on What Works Best for Your Child

Use the prompts below to help guide your thoughts around a custody schedule:

- What parts of their routine feel especially important to keep consistent?

- Are there any current transitions (pick-ups, drop-offs, etc.) that feel stressful?

- What days/times does your child seem most relaxed and connected?

- Who handles which parts of their routine now—and will that need to shift?

Step 3: Custody Schedule Considerations

Custody Option	*Pros for My Child*	*Potential Challenges*
Week-on / Week-off		
2-2-3 Schedule		
Every Other Weekend		
Custom Hybrid (describe below)		

What does least disruptive and most nurturing look like for your child—and for you?

Find the Experts you need at freshstartsregistry.com/experts

What Factors Do Courts Consider When Determining Custody?

While every family is different, most courts base custody decisions on what's considered the "best interest of the child." This includes emotional bonds, school schedules, each parent's caregiving history, and each parent's ability to provide a safe and supportive environment. It's not about punishing one parent or rewarding another—it's about setting your child up for the most stable outcome.

Questions to Ask: What are my child's emotional, educational, and developmental needs right now? What has been each parent's role in caregiving so far? Can I demonstrate my ability to co-parent cooperatively and responsibly?

Action Step: Begin collecting documentation that shows your involvement in your child's life—school forms, medical records, messages with teachers, or photos of daily routines. These can help demonstrate your role and commitment if custody becomes contested.

How Can We Minimize Conflict for the Sake of the Kids?

Children are sensitive to stress and tension, especially between parents. While divorce can be hard, it doesn't have to be traumatic. Kids benefit most from peaceful, respectful co-parenting—whether that's through parallel parenting, structured communication, or clear boundaries.

Questions to Ask: How can we reduce the emotional burden on our children during this process? What rules and communication strategies will help minimize conflict? What kind of support do I need to model emotional regulation for my kids?

Action Step: Establish a co-parenting communication plan using apps like OurFamilyWizard or TalkingParents, which help create structure and reduce the potential for miscommunication. Begin practicing emotional boundaries during interactions with your ex, especially when your children are present.

How Is Child Support Calculated, and What Do I Need to Know?

Child support is typically calculated based on income, time spent with each parent, and the needs of the child. Each state has its own formula. The goal is to ensure that children's basic needs are met and that both parents contribute fairly.

Question to Ask: Do I understand how child support is calculated in my state, and what documentation I need to prepare?

Action Step: Look up your state's child support guidelines and calculator. Gather income statements, childcare expenses, and health insurance information to begin estimating what payments might look like.

What Will Child Support Cover—and What Won't It?

Child support is designed to cover essentials—food, clothing, housing, and basic care. But many expenses fall outside that category, like extracurriculars, school supplies, or uncovered medical bills. Being clear about who pays for what will help avoid future confusion.

Question to Ask: Are there shared expenses (like sports, therapy, or tutoring) that we need to address separately from monthly support?

Action Step: Make a list of recurring child-related costs outside of basic needs. Discuss how you and your co-parent will divide those expenses and whether you want to include them in your written parenting plan.

How Do We Handle Holidays, School Breaks, and Big Life Decisions?

Even the most amicable custody agreements can get complicated during holidays, summer vacations, or milestone decisions like education or religion. Planning ahead prevents conflict and gives children the benefit of predictable structure and shared joy.

Questions to Ask: What are our non-negotiables when it comes to holidays and special occasions? How do we want to approach long-term decisions like school choice, healthcare, or travel? Are we willing to revisit and adjust our custody agreement as the children grow?

Action Step: Draft a holiday and special event calendar for the next year. Note major dates and think about what would be most supportive for your child—and workable for you. Bring this calendar to custody discussions or mediation sessions as a tool.

Moving Forward

Custody decisions are deeply emotional—but they're also an opportunity to build a foundation of safety, routine, and resilience for your children. By asking the right questions, centering your child's needs, and approaching this process with compassion and preparation, you're taking powerful steps to support their future.

Co-Parenting Plan Worksheet

Purpose: This worksheet is designed to help co-parents create a clear, structured agreement that supports your children's well-being, minimizes conflict, and promotes consistency across both households.

Custody & Visitation Schedule

Physical Custody Schedule

Weekdays: _____

Weekends: _____

Holidays: _____

School Breaks: _____

Birthdays/Special Occasions: _____

Legal Custody Agreement (Who makes major decisions for the child?)

Education: _____

Medical: _____

Religion: _____

Extracurriculars: _____

Communication Plan

Preferred Method(s) of Communication

☐ Email ☐ Text ☐ Phone Calls ☐ Other: _____

☐ Co-parenting app (e.g., OurFamilyWizard): _____

Response Time Expectations: We agree to respond within _____ hours/days.

Conflict Resolution Plan

If a disagreement arises, we will:

☐ Mediate between ourselves

☐ Use a professional mediator

☐ Consult a therapist/coach

☐ Other:_____

Household Guidelines

Consistency Between Homes

(e.g., bedtime routines, homework expectations, screen time limits)

_____

_____

_____

Discipline Approach:

_____

_____

_____

Religious Practices (if applicable):

_____

_____

_____

Decision-Making Protocols

How will major decisions be made?

☐ Jointly with discussion ☐ Primary parent makes decisions

☐ Alternate decision-making (e.g., Parent A handles education, Parent B handles healthcare)

Notes: _____

_____

How will emergency decisions be handled?

_____

_____

_____

Emergency & Contact Info

Backup Contact if Parent is Unreachable:

_____

Medical Emergency Plan: _____

_____

School Contact Plan: _____

_____

Child Support Estimator Worksheet

Purpose: This worksheet will help you organize financial details, understand what impacts support amounts, and estimate what child support may look like in your case.

STEP 1: Identify State Guidelines

State You're Filing In: _____

Does your state use a standard calculator or percentage model?

(Google "your state + child support model")

☐ **Income Shares Model**

☐ **Percentage of Obligor's Income**

☐ **Other (write in):** _____

STEP 2: Income Information

Your Monthly Gross Income (Before Taxes): $_____

Other Parent's Monthly Gross Income: $_____

Other income to include (bonuses, side jobs, etc.):

Total Combined Gross Income (Monthly): $_____

STEP 3: Child-Related Expenses

Number of Children Shared: _____

Monthly Childcare Costs: $_____

Health Insurance Premiums for Child(ren): $_____

Out-of-Pocket Medical Expenses: $_____

Educational/Extracurricular Costs: $_____

Do you split these expenses?

☐ **50/50** ☐ **Proportional to income** ☐ **Other (explain):** _____

STEP 4: Estimate Child Support

Most states have online calculators available, take all of the information you've compiled and Google "your state + child support calculator" and input to see the results.

Estimated Monthly Child Support Obligation: $_____

Paid by: _____ **to** _____.

(based on calculator or attorney input)

STEP 5: Notes & Legal Follow-Up

Questions to Ask a Lawyer or Mediator:

What is the typical child support amount for my income level and parenting time?

How does our custody schedule impact support?

Next Steps:

☐ Schedule a meeting with a family lawyer

☐ Research your state's support guidelines

☐ Gather pay stubs, tax returns, and bank statements

☐ Prepare for mediation or court

_____

_____

_____

_____

_____

CHAPTER 17

Co-Parenting, Parallel Parenting, and Navigating Blended Families

Once custody agreements are in place, the real work begins: showing up consistently for your children in a new structure, with new boundaries and new dynamics. Whether you're building a co-parenting relationship, creating space through parallel parenting, or integrating new partners into a blended family, this chapter is about the day-to-day reality of raising children after divorce.

There's no single right way to do this. Every family is different. What matters most is that you make decisions rooted in what's healthiest and most stable for your children—and for you.

What Kind of Parenting Relationship Are We Capable Of Right Now?

One of the first decisions to make after divorce is what kind of parenting dynamic you and your ex can realistically maintain. Co-parenting requires open communication and mutual respect. Parallel parenting, on the other hand, creates more distance and structure—often used when direct communication leads to conflict.

Questions to Ask: Can we communicate respectfully without conflict? Are we aligned on key parenting values and decisions? What kind of structure would reduce tension and protect our child's well-being?

Action Step: Identify what kind of contact with your co-parent feels manageable right now. If communication is high-conflict, consider a parallel parenting model with structured routines and communication apps to minimize direct contact.

How Do We Prioritize the Kids When Emotions Are High?

Post-divorce emotions are real and valid—but they can't take center stage in your parenting. The ability to separate your personal hurt from your parenting responsibilities is one of the most important skills you can develop in this season.

Questions to Ask: What am I modeling for my kids when I talk about my co-parent? How can I create an emotionally safe environment for my child, even when I'm hurting? What do my kids need from both of us to feel secure and loved?

Action Step: Choose a phrase you'll use to stay neutral when discussing your co-parent with your child—for example, "That's something you'll talk to Dad about," or "Your mom loves you very much." This protects your child's emotional space while keeping your boundaries clear.

What Boundaries Are Needed Between Homes?

Children thrive with predictability, even across two different households. That doesn't mean both homes need to be identical—but it does mean establishing a few shared agreements, and accepting where flexibility is more realistic than uniformity.

Questions to Ask: What rules or routines would benefit from consistency in both homes? Where can I let go of control for the sake of peace? What is within my control in my home that promotes stability?

Action Step: Write down the top three routines that matter most to you—like bedtime, screen time, or mealtime expectations. Talk to your co-parent about whether there's room for overlap. Then, let go of the rest. Control what you can, and model flexibility for your child.

How Do We Navigate New Relationships and Blended Families?

Introducing new partners or merging families is a major transition, and timing matters. Children need time to adjust to the loss of their previous family structure before they can fully welcome new ones. Respecting their pace, validating their feelings, and communicating clearly can make all the difference.

Questions to Ask: Is my child ready to meet a new partner—and am I? How can I communicate about new relationships with honesty and compassion? What kind of support does my child need as family dynamics evolve?

Action Step: If you're entering a blended family, talk to a family therapist or read together with your child about stepfamilies. Prepare them in advance, answer their questions honestly, and maintain your own consistency so they feel grounded.

Moving Forward

Parenting after divorce is a long game. It's not about perfection—it's about presence. Whether you're co-parenting in harmony, parallel parenting with structure, or building a new blended life, your goal is to lead with steadiness and love. Your child doesn't need a flawless plan—they need a connected parent. And that's exactly what you're becoming.

CHAPTER 18

—————

Your Health, Mental Health, and Self-Care

Let's be honest—when everything's falling apart, taking care of yourself can feel like the last thing on the list. You're juggling paperwork, parenting, finances, and just trying to get through the day. But here's the truth: your well-being matters more than ever right now. This season will ask a lot of you, and you deserve to feel supported, steady, and strong in your own body and mind.

In this chapter, we're inviting you to check in with yourself—not in a bubble bath, face-mask kind of way (unless that helps!), but in a real, grounded way. We'll walk through the questions that help you reconnect with what you need, protect your mental health, and build self-care routines that actually work in your real life. Because the person at the center of all this change? They deserve care too.

How Is My Body Responding to Stress Right Now?

Divorce often triggers intense physical symptoms: tension headaches, sleep disruption, digestive issues, fatigue, even a racing heart. These are normal responses to stress—but they're also messages from your body asking for care.

Questions to Ask: Am I eating regularly and staying hydrated? How is my sleep— do I feel rested or depleted? Where in my body am I holding tension or anxiety?

Action Step: Choose one simple thing you can do today to respond to your body's needs. That might mean drinking water, stretching your back, taking a nap, or getting outside for ten minutes. Let this be a signal to your nervous system that you are safe and supported.

What's Supporting—or Draining—My Mental Health?

This is an emotionally complex time. You might be cycling through grief, fear, relief, anger, and confusion—sometimes all in one day. Naming what's helping and what's hurting your mental health allows you to make adjustments with intention and compassion.

Questions to Ask: What activities, people, or habits leave me feeling calm and centered? What drains me emotionally or sends me into a spiral? Do I have tools or practices I can lean on when the waves hit?

Action Step: Make two columns labeled "Supportive" and "Draining." Fill them in honestly. Then choose one thing from the Supportive list to add into your week— and one from the Draining list to reduce or remove.

Self-Care Check-In Worksheet

Step 1: Name What's Lifting You Up and What's Wearing You Down

Take a few quiet minutes to reflect. What's helping you feel grounded, hopeful, or even just a little lighter? What's leaving you depleted, overwhelmed, or disconnected?

Supportive	Draining (in a bad way)

Self-Care Check-In Worksheet

Step 2: Choose with Intention

Pick one thing from your Supportive list to lean into this week. Circle it, schedule it, or make space for it—even if it's just 10 minutes.

Pick one thing from your Draining list to reduce, delegate, or release—just for now.

Supportive thing I'll add or lean into this week:

_____

_____

Draining thing I'll reduce or let go of this week:

_____

_____

Gentle Reflection

What would it feel like to give myself permission to need support?

_____

How can I remind myself that small shifts count?

_____

What's one way I can celebrate showing up for myself this week?

_____

Am I Getting the Support I Need?

You don't have to carry this alone. Support can look like therapy, group coaching, medication, breathwork, journaling, or just venting to a trusted friend. There is no gold star for doing this all by yourself—just burnout. Support is strength.

Questions to Ask: Do I have at least one person I can talk to without judgment? Would working with a therapist or coach give me space to process? What kind of support feels most nourishing right now—emotional, physical, spiritual?

Action Step: If you haven't already, research local or online therapists who specialize in divorce, trauma, or life transitions. Schedule a consultation, or reach out to a friend and let them know you need extra support this week.

How Can I Create a Self-Care Routine That's Actually Realistic?

Self-care doesn't need to be elaborate or time-consuming. It can look like a five-minute morning ritual, saying no to something that drains you, or moving your body in a way that feels good. The key is making it realistic enough that you'll actually do it.

Questions to Ask: What makes me feel like myself again—even briefly? What kind of routine would feel supportive, not overwhelming? How can I build self-care into what I'm already doing each day?

Action Step: Choose one small ritual to try for the next week—like making tea in silence, taking a morning walk, journaling one sentence at night, or setting a "do not disturb" hour each day. Start small, and let consistency build trust with yourself.

Moving Forward

Taking care of yourself during divorce isn't selfish—it's essential. You're navigating one of life's most demanding transitions. Your body and mind are carrying a heavy load. By tending to your health and mental well-being now, you're not just surviving—you're building a foundation for the next chapter of your life. And you deserve to feel held, supported, and whole along the way.

——

CHAPTER 19

Managing Expectations – Yours, Theirs, and Everyone Else's

You might notice it quietly—or all at once: the opinions, the advice, the side comments wrapped in concern. People around you may suddenly have a lot to say about your divorce, your timeline, your healing. And then there's your own inner voice, tangled up in ideas about how this should feel or where you should be by now.

If any of that sounds familiar, take a deep breath—you're not alone. This chapter is a space to lay it all down. Together, we'll sort through the noise, get clear on what actually matters to you, and gently release anything that doesn't belong. You get to decide what this season looks like. Let's start there.

What Expectations Am I Placing on Myself?

You may be expecting yourself to stay strong, keep everything together, not miss a beat at work, or never cry in front of your kids. These internal pressures are often shaped by cultural messaging, past experiences, or perfectionism. But here's the truth: you are allowed to fall apart, feel lost, and not have it all figured out right now.

Questions to Ask: Am I holding myself to unrealistic standards right now? What would it feel like to give myself permission to be human? If my best friend were in my shoes, what would I say to her?

Action Step: Write yourself a permission slip. It might say: "I give myself permission to rest." Or "I give myself permission to not have all the answers yet." Post it somewhere visible. Let it be your reminder that grace is a strength.

What Do Others Expect of Me, and How Do I Want to Respond?

Friends and family may mean well, but sometimes their questions, opinions, or expectations can feel heavy or intrusive. You might hear things like "Aren't you over it yet?" or "You should just..." Their expectations are not your responsibility to meet. Your healing timeline is your own.

Questions to Ask: Whose voice is influencing me right now—and do I agree with it? Am I doing something to earn someone else's approval, or because it's what I truly want? How can I lovingly hold a boundary when others push?

Action Step: Choose a response you can use when others offer unsolicited advice or judgment. Something like, "I appreciate your concern, but I'm making the choices that feel right for me." Practice saying it until it feels steady in your mouth.

Find the Experts you need at freshstartsregistry.com/experts

What Do I Expect This Season to Look Like—and Is That Realistic?

Maybe you expected the divorce process to be faster, smoother, less emotional. Or maybe you thought you'd feel more relieved—or less alone. Unmet expectations can create grief or guilt, even if your decisions were right for you. Honoring reality instead of fighting it can create the spaciousness you need to heal.

Questions to Ask: What did I think this season would look like, and what has been different? What am I grieving that I didn't even realize I'd miss? Can I meet this season as it is, not as I thought it would be?

Action Step: Write a letter to the version of you who thought things would go differently. Thank her for her hopes. Then write a second letter to the version of you who is here now. Welcome her. Let her know she is not failing—she is adapting.

How Can I Start Defining Success on My Own Terms?

Letting go of other people's expectations opens the door to defining your own version of success. Maybe success means getting out of bed each day. Maybe it's building a new life, one boundary and one joy at a time. Your story is not meant to look like anyone else's—and that's the beauty of it.

Questions to Ask: What does success look like for me in this chapter? What makes me feel proud, grounded, or free? How can I celebrate even the smallest wins?

Action Step: Write a new definition of success for yourself. It could be a single sentence: "Success is staying true to myself." Or "Success is building a peaceful home." Let that definition guide your next steps—not someone else's timeline.

Moving Forward

Managing expectations—especially your own—isn't about doing more. It's about releasing what was never yours to carry. Divorce is not a performance, and healing is not a race. The more you can tune into your own voice, the more empowered you'll feel in every part of this process. You're allowed to take your time. You're allowed to make it yours.

CHAPTER 20

Empowering Yourself Through Knowledge and Community Support

One of the most difficult parts of divorce is the feeling that you're doing it alone. So much of this experience happens behind closed doors—late-night searches, quiet tears, and moments of doubt. But you are not alone. And you don't have to figure everything out by yourself.

Empowerment during divorce doesn't mean having all the answers. It means knowing where to find them. It means connecting with people who understand. It means realizing that asking for help is a strength, not a weakness. In this chapter, we'll explore how knowledge and community can be your lifelines—and your launchpads—as you move through and beyond divorce.

Where Can I Find Reliable Information About Divorce?

There's a lot of misinformation out there, especially online. But good, accurate, trustworthy knowledge exists—and it can help you make decisions with confidence. Knowing your rights, understanding your options, and learning the process makes the unknown feel less scary.

Questions to Ask: Do I understand the laws and timelines specific to divorce in my state? Am I relying on reliable sources—or social media opinions? What do I still feel unsure or overwhelmed about?

Action Step: Write down a list of the areas where you feel unclear—finances, custody, legal steps, etc. Then, seek out resources from trusted professionals or platforms that prioritize education and support. Our free e-book, Your Divorce Support Team: 250+ Questions to Help You Build Your Divorce Support Team, is a great place to start.

Who Can I Turn to for Support Without Judgment?

Divorce can feel isolating. You may have lost mutual friends, or you may not want to burden loved ones. But you deserve connection. You deserve to be witnessed. Surrounding yourself with people who listen, affirm, and encourage you makes all the difference. You can also connect with our CEO, Olivia Howell, who offers one-on-one conversations to listen without judgment and help refer you to the right experts and resources. She's here to support you in building your fresh start.

Questions to Ask: Who in my life can hold space for me without judgment or unsolicited advice? Are there support groups or communities where I can connect with others going through divorce? Do I need professional help—like a therapist, coach, or mentor—to guide me through this?

Action Step: Reach out to one person today who feels emotionally safe. You don't have to share everything—just start the connection. Also consider joining an online or in-person support group for people navigating divorce. It's powerful to be surrounded by people who get it.

How Can I Stay Informed Without Becoming Overwhelmed?

It's easy to go down a research rabbit hole—and wind up more confused than when you started. Empowerment comes from intentional, focused learning. You don't need to become a legal expert. You just need to be informed enough to advocate for yourself.

Questions to Ask: What's the one thing I need to understand better this week? Am I reading to gain clarity—or feeding my anxiety? What would it look like to pace myself and protect my peace?

Action Step: Choose one topic to research this week—just one. Maybe it's custody laws, how to write a parenting plan, or what to expect at a mediation. Set a time limit, take notes, and then step away. Let the information settle before jumping to the next topic.

How Can I Give Back—or Reach Back—When I'm Ready?

You may not be there yet—and that's okay. But one day, you'll look back and realize how far you've come. And you may feel called to help others who are starting where you once stood. Empowerment is a ripple effect. Community is built on courage shared.

Questions to Ask: Who helped me feel less alone in this process? What would I say to someone just beginning their divorce journey? How can I use my experience to make someone else's road a little lighter?

Action Step: Write down three things you've learned through this process so far. Save them. When you're ready, consider sharing your story with someone who needs it. Your voice could be the light someone else is looking for.

Moving Forward

Empowerment doesn't come from doing everything perfectly. It comes from knowing you can handle whatever comes next because you've built support around you. Knowledge gives you options. Community gives you strength. And together, they give you the power to begin again.

CHAPTER 21

Preparing for Life After Divorce— Rebuilding and Moving Forward

Divorce might close one chapter, but it doesn't mean the story is over—it just means you're turning the page. This isn't the end of your life, it's a shift, a transition, a beginning you didn't expect but now get to shape. Once the logistics settle, you're left with something both tender and powerful: the chance to ask, what do I want now?

In this chapter, we'll gently walk through what it means to rebuild with intention. You don't need to have all the answers—you just need enough space to imagine what's next, and the support to take the first few steps forward.

What Kind of Life Do I Want to Build Next?

You've spent months—or years—unwinding from a shared life. Now, you get to imagine what you want to create. This is your time to dream, even if it feels scary or unfamiliar. Your values, your rhythms, and your needs get to be the blueprint.

Questions to Ask: What did I miss most when I was in survival mode? What brings me peace, joy, or a sense of purpose? If nothing was holding me back, what would I try, start, or create?

Action Step: Take an hour to sit down and journal or make a vision board. Don't worry about how it will happen—just focus on what you want your life to feel like. That feeling is your guide.

What Do I Want Home to Feel Like Now?

One powerful way to support this process is by creating a divorce registry through Fresh Starts. A divorce registry allows you to build your new home intentionally and with support—whether you need basics like kitchenware or comfort items that bring you peace. It's a practical and emotional tool to help you rebuild your space on your terms, and invite others to support you in meaningful ways.

You're not just redefining your relationship—you're redefining your space. Whether you stayed in the family home or moved to a new one, this is your chance to make your environment feel safe, cozy, and uniquely yours. You get to choose what stays, what goes, and what energy you want to welcome in.

Questions to Ask: What objects or rooms still carry the emotional weight of the past? What makes me feel grounded and at ease in my space? Is there a small ritual I can begin to reconnect with my home and myself?

Action Step: Pick one room, drawer, or corner to reclaim. Clean it out. Rearrange it. Add something new—a candle, a print, a plant. Let it symbolize your fresh start.

How Do I Reconnect with Myself and My Identity?

Divorce often comes with an identity shift. Who are you now, outside of that relationship? What parts of yourself are reemerging—or just beginning to show up for the first time? You don't need all the answers today. You just need to stay curious.

Questions to Ask: What did I love before the relationship that I want to rediscover? What kind of routines or rituals help me feel like myself? How can I begin to trust myself again?

Action Step: Make a list of small things you can do this month just for you—reading a book, joining a class, trying a new recipe, or going somewhere alone. Follow your interests. Let yourself explore.

What Support Do I Need Moving Forward?

You don't need to go into this next chapter alone. Support isn't just for the crisis stage—it's for rebuilding, too. Whether it's a therapist, a friend, a coach, or a community, surrounding yourself with people who uplift you is essential.

Questions to Ask: Who in my life truly supports my growth and peace? What kind of encouragement or accountability would help me stay focused on my goals? How can I continue investing in my healing?

Action Step: Schedule one support-focused appointment this month. That could be therapy, coaching, or even just a coffee with a friend who always lifts you up. You deserve to feel held as you move forward.

Moving Forward

Life after divorce isn't about starting over from scratch—it's about building forward from who you are now. With each decision, each routine, and each act of care, you are laying the foundation for a life that reflects your strength, your wisdom, and your joy. You get to begin again—and this time, you get to do it on your own terms.

CHAPTER 22

Finding Peace with Your Decision

Making the decision to divorce is one of the most deeply personal—and often most agonizing—choices a person can make. Even if you know it's the right decision, the emotional aftermath can still feel confusing and heavy. It's common to wonder if you did the right thing, if you tried hard enough, or if you could have done something differently. This chapter is about making space for those questions, honoring your experience, and allowing peace to emerge—gently, over time.

What Feelings Are Still Lingering?

Closure isn't something someone else gives you—it's something you allow yourself. That often begins with naming the feelings you're still carrying. Guilt. Anger. Relief. Loneliness. Hope. Letting yourself feel all of it, without judgment, is part of the healing process.

Questions to Ask: What emotions come up when I think about my decision? Have I given myself permission to feel grief, even if I'm also relieved? Am I holding onto any shame that isn't mine to carry?

Action Step: Set aside a quiet moment to write down what you're still holding onto. Then ask yourself: what do I want to let go of today? Create a small ritual to release it—a walk, a tearful exhale, a candle, a bath. Rituals remind your nervous system: it's safe to let go.

How Can I Begin to Trust Myself Again?

Divorce can shake your sense of confidence. You may doubt your instincts or worry that your choices hurt others. But trust isn't about perfection—it's about listening, adjusting, and staying rooted in your truth, even when it's hard.

Questions to Ask: What values guided my decision to leave—or to stay as long as I did? When have I honored myself, even in small ways, during this process? What would it look like to treat myself with the same compassion I offer others?

Action Step: Make a list of three hard things you've done in this process that you're proud of. Let that be your evidence that you can trust yourself. You have already done brave things.

What Does Peace Look Like for Me?

Peace won't look like it does in movies. It won't arrive all at once with a bow on top. It might show up quietly—in a deep breath, in a moment of stillness, in a full night of sleep. Your peace is yours to define, and it will unfold slowly, as you continue to move forward.

Questions to Ask: What helps me feel most at ease in my body and mind? Where do I notice peace showing up, even in small moments? What boundaries or habits can I create to protect my peace?

Action Step: Create a "peace menu" you can return to—small, accessible things that bring you calm. Maybe it's a playlist, a walk, a poem, a trusted voice. These tools help you return to yourself when life feels loud.

Moving Forward

Finding peace with your decision isn't about being 100% certain every day—it's about knowing you made the best choice you could with the information, strength, and heart you had at the time. It's about trusting that you are allowed to begin again. You don't have to rush toward peace. Just keep moving gently in its direction. One choice, one boundary, one breath at a time.

Peace Menu Worksheet

Step 1: What Brings You Calm?

Think about the moments when you've felt a little more grounded—even for a second. What helped? Use the prompts below to build your personalized "Peace Menu."

Category	Peaceful Tools & Practices
Sounds & Music	playlists, nature sounds, certain voices
Words	poems, quotes, affirmations, books
Movement	walks, stretching, dancing, deep breaths
Sensory Anchors	candles, warm tea, textures, smells
People & Support	a friend, therapist, hotline, spiritual guide
Grounding Practices	journaling, meditating, sitting in the sun
Tiny Joys	fresh flowers, a favorite snack, 10-minute naps

Step 2: Choose 3 Go-To Tools for Hard Moments

Write down three calming tools you want to try first when things feel loud or overwhelming:

1. _____

2. _____

3. _____

Step 3: Keep It Visible

Where can you keep this menu so you'll actually use it?

☐ **Journal** ☐ **Fridge or mirror** ☐ **Shared with a friend or therapist**

☐ **Phone notes** ☐ **Printed copy in your bag**

Find the Experts you need at freshstartsregistry.com/experts

Finding Support Through Fresh Starts Registry

At Fresh Starts Registry, we know that divorce is about more than paperwork. It's about rebuilding your life—emotionally, practically, and spiritually. That's why we've created a community-centered platform to walk with you through every step of your fresh start.

We offer tangible and emotional support for people navigating divorce and major life transitions. Whether you're still in the consideration phase or well into your new chapter, you don't have to do this alone.

What We Offer

The World's First Divorce Registry

You can create a registry of practical and supportive items—everything from bedsheets to books to blenders—so your friends and family can show up for you in meaningful ways. It's about celebrating your next chapter and giving you the tools to rebuild your home and life.

Expert Guidance and Referrals

We've built a trusted directory of vetted divorce professionals—from attorneys and therapists to financial advisors and real estate agents. These experts are here to support you with clarity and compassion. Need a personal referral? Reach out directly to our CEO, Olivia Howell, for a free support call.

Free Education and Resources

Our growing library of free e-books, guides, blog posts, and podcast episodes cover everything from parenting plans to financial prep to co-parenting etiquette. We believe education should be accessible—because knowledge is empowerment.

Community and Encouragement

Join our Instagram community @freshstartsregistry for daily support, real stories, and inspiration from people who have been exactly where you are. You'll also find updates on workshops, community events, and new resources.

Get in Touch

Visit us at freshstartsregistry.com to explore the full platform.

Follow along on Instagram @freshstartsregistry

Email us anytime at hi@freshstartsregistry.com

You deserve support. You deserve celebration. You deserve a fresh start.

We're here to walk beside you.